on track ...
Badfinger

every album, every song

Robert Day-Webb

sonicbondpublishing.com

Sonicbond Publishing Limited
www.sonicbondpublishing.co.uk
Email: info@sonicbondpublishing.co.uk

First Published in the United Kingdom 2022
First Published in the United States 2022

British Library Cataloguing in Publication Data:
A Catalogue record for this book is available from the British Library

Typeset in ITC Garamond & ITC Avant Garde
Printed and bound in England

Graphic design and typesetting: Full Moon Media

Acknowledgements

I would like to dedicate this book, with love, to my family:
Rie, Josh, Lolly, Matt and Dan.

I would also like to say a big thank you to Stephen Lambe at
Sonicbond, not only for the opportunity to write this book but also
for all the help, guidance and patience.

Huge thanks also to all the people out there who have previously
carried out the invaluable research utilised within this book,
particularly the following individuals:
Dan Matovina, whose biographical tome on Badfinger was an
indispensable resource (*Without You: The Tragic Story of Badfinger* –
Frances Glover Books, 1997; second edition 2000).

Tom Brennan and his truly phenomenal *Badfinger Library* website
which provided additional and up-to-date information.

Michael A. Cimino, for his book, *Badfinger and Beyond – The
Biography of Joey Molland* (Cottage Views, 2011) which provided
valuable information from Joey Molland's perspective.

Finally, of course, the biggest thank you of all goes out to Pete, Tom,
Joey and Mike (and, indeed, everyone else who passed through the
ranks of Badfinger) for the wonderful music you created.
Without You…

Would you like to write for Sonicbond Publishing?
We are mainly a music publisher, but we also occasionally publish in other genres including film and television. At Sonicbond Publishing we are always on the look-out for authors, particularly for our two main series, On Track and Decades.

Mixing fact with in depth analysis, the On Track series examines the entire recorded work of a particular musical artist or group. All genres are considered from easy listening and jazz to 60s soul to 90s pop, via rock and metal.

The Decades series singles out a particular decade in an artist or group's history and focuses on that decade in more detail than may be allowed in the On Track series.

While professional writing experience would, of course, be an advantage, the most important qualification is to have real enthusiasm and knowledge of your subject. First-time authors are welcomed, but the ability to write well in English is essential.

Sonicbond Publishing has distribution throughout Europe and North America, and all our books are also published in E-book form. Authors will be paid a royalty based on sales of their book. Further details about our books are available from www.sonicbondpublishing.com. To contact us, complete the contact form there or email info@sonicbondpublishing.co.uk

on track ...

Badfinger

Contents

Introduction

The story of Badfinger is famously renowned for being one of the most tragic in all of rock 'n' roll history. Indeed, they are possibly more well-known for their devastatingly ruinous trials and tribulations than their actual music. Whilst their tale is certainly a cautionary one rife with examples of abysmal and shameful management, complex and seemingly unending legal proceedings and persistent financial problems, all culminating in the dreadful suicides of two of the band's main protagonists, it should not be allowed to overshadow their musical legacy.

Frequently touted back in the day as 'the next Beatles,' 'the new Fab Four'and other similar Beatle-comparing labels, Badfinger were global superstars-in-waiting. They were the very first act signed to The Beatles' Apple Records label (albeit in their pre-Badfinger guise, The Iveys) and enjoyed a run of four consecutive worldwide hit singles in the early 1970s (the first of which was the Paul McCartney-penned 'Come And Get It', followed by 'No Matter What', 'Day After Day' and 'Baby Blue'). They reportedly went on to sell fourteen million albums worldwide and with the track 'Without You', co-written by band members Pete Ham and Tom Evans, they also created a true classic pop standard which has subsequently been covered by numerous artists, most notably by Harry Nilsson and Mariah Carey, who both scored global number one hits with their respective versions of the song.

The band's classic line-up of Pete Ham, Tom Evans, Joey Molland and Mike Gibbins shared a unique and magical chemistry, and two of their albums in particular, *Straight Up* and *Wish You Were Here*, are frequently hailed by critics as genuine classics. Inextricably linked with The Beatles, members of Badfinger even found themselves playing on their patrons' solo LPs – George Harrison's *All Things Must Pass* and John Lennon's *Imagine*.

Whilst managerial, legal and financial issues ultimately put paid to any chances of the band fulfilling their true potential at the time, their music has posthumously endured, and to this day, it continues to reach out and touch fans across the world. Indeed, as recently as 2013, a whole new generation of fans discovered the band via their track 'Baby Blue', which was used in the final ever episode of cult US TV drama, *Breaking Bad*. Within this book, I shall take an analytical look at every official album and track they released in their lifetime (including their pre-Badfinger incarnation, The Iveys) whilst also offering some insight into what was happening behind the scenes during the respective album periods in order to flesh out their story. I will, therefore, inevitably touch upon the various managerial, financial and legal woes that the band endured, but since the specific focus of this book is on the actual music, I would direct interested readers to other related tomes that delve much deeper and more comprehensively into the complex web of business shenanigans that continually plagued the band (such as Dan Matovina's superlative band biography). My primary aim here is to shine a light on their musical legacy with an honest and truthful critical analysis of their recorded output. Hopefully, fans old and new will enjoy reading the following pages and, afterwards, if it sends you scurrying off to investigate the Badfinger songbook further, then I will consider my work well and truly done!

[Note: All US chart placings within the book refer to the *Billboard* 200 chart (for albums) and the *Billboard* Hot 100 (for singles); all UK chart data is sourced from the Official UK Charts Company.]

Prologue

The origin of the Badfinger story can be traced back to South Wales (UK) in the early 1960s, when Swansea native and budding musician, Pete Ham (born 27 April 1947), formed a band initially called The Panthers. Over the next few years, the band's line-up and moniker changed several times until 1964, whereupon the band, now centred around the core line-up of Pete Ham (guitar), Ron Griffiths (bass guitar) and David 'Dai' Jenkins (rhythm guitar), settled upon the name The Iveys (which had been inspired by several reasons – Ivey Place, a small street in Swansea, the song 'Poison Ivy' which the band were fond of, and the fact that the moniker made for a pleasing association with The Hollies, a band for whom they had much admiration). They acquired a new drummer in 1965 in the form of one Mike Gibbins, another Swansea-bred lad (born 12 March 1949).

The following year, a gentleman by the name of Bill Collins took a shine to the band and, seeing a lot of potential in the boys, became their manager (interestingly, Bill Collins was the father of future film and TV actor Lewis Collins, who later found fame in the late 1970s/early 1980s playing 'Bodie' in the British TV show, *The Professionals*). Bill soon convinced the band to relocate to London in order to seriously pursue their musical career and so, by the second half of 1966, the band members found themselves ensconced in Park Avenue, Golders Green, London, not too far from Abbey Road Studios. Once settled in London, the band fervently set about writing and recording demos and gigging. Even at this early stage, Pete Ham displayed a lot of promise in the songwriting department, so much so that Kinks leader Ray Davies even wanted to produce them (in actual fact, he ended up producing three demos with the band). By the end of 1966, Bill Collins had officially formalised his position with the band by signing a management contract with the boys.

Around August 1967, Dai Jenkins was replaced by Liverpudlian musician Tom Evans (born 5 June 1947), and by 1968, all four band members were writing and contributing material with their compositions all tending towards melodically-oriented pop songs. By this time, they were also a fairly successful live act and the lads were beginning to build up a decent following.

On the back of their growing popularity, Bill Collins managed to attract the interest of one Mal Evans, famed Beatles roadie and friend. Mal liked what he heard and decided to take some demos back to the recently Beatle-formed Apple corporation for the attention of the powers that be (including the Beatles themselves). Mal relentlessly promoted the band at Apple and eventually convinced the Apple bosses to sign The Iveys. The band were duly signed to Apple Records in July 1968, in the process becoming the first non-Beatle act to be signed to the label. In addition to the record deal, the band also signed a publishing contract with Apple Music in October 1968. Subsequently, a sense of euphoria naturally pervaded the jubilant band's camp at this time and the world was seemingly theirs for the taking...

Maybe Tomorrow

Personnel:
Pete Ham: vocals, lead guitar, keyboards
Tom Evans: vocals, rhythm guitar
Ron Griffiths: vocals, bass guitar
Mike Gibbins: vocals, drums, percussion
Recorded at Trident, Olympic and Morgan Studios, London, UK (July 1968 – March 1969)
Produced and arranged by Tony Visconti except for * produced by Mal Evans and arranged by John Barham and Mal Evans
Not released in US or UK (only released in Italy, Germany and Japan: September 1969)

Almost immediately after signing with Apple, the band entered Trident Studios in Soho, London, and set about recording some of their material. Initially, Denny Cordell (who'd worked with the likes of The Moody Blues, Procol Harum and The Move) was assigned as producer, but due to ongoing production commitments elsewhere, he was replaced after just one day by his assistant Tony Visconti (who was also working with Marc Bolan/Tyrannosaurus Rex and David Bowie at the time). These first few months of recording sessions saw the band attempt to find a potential hit single. They ended up recording several good, solid numbers (all self-penned by respective band members), but none of them leapt out as being an obvious choice for that all-important first single.

It wasn't until they attempted Tom Evans' 'Maybe Tomorrow' that they discovered they were onto something very promising. Visconti subsequently weaved his production and arrangement magic on the track and Apple duly approved of the completed song and confirmed that it would be the band's debut single. A promotional film was also shot for the track, which featured the youthful and fresh-faced foursome, dressed in matching suits, lip-syncing to the song. Whilst the single was being prepped for release, the band remained busy, spending their time either recording, rehearsing or performing live gigs. November 1968 saw the release of the 'Maybe Tomorrow' single in the UK, accompanied by some decent reviews in the music press. *Disc and Music Echo* had this to say:

> This is as good as you could wish – very gentle, very warm, super lead singer who sounds like McCartney and very, very pretty.

The *New Musical Express* (*NME*) was almost as positive in its review:

> This is a pungent beat-ballad with a rather wistful lyric ... pleasant vocal blend, though I thought the soloist's exaggerated soul contributions were a little overdone. And the gorgeous stringy scoring is positively scintillating.

However, overall, the promotional campaign was a little lacking (mainly due to internal issues at Apple), and by mid-December it became apparent that the song was not going to be a hit in the domestic market. Pete Ham later shared his thoughts on the song's domestic chart failure (in the *Magic Christian Music* songbook, 1970):

> I was brought down when our first record with Apple, which was 'Maybe Tomorrow', didn't do anything. The trouble was, we were stupid and we sat back and thought it would just happen. And it didn't.

Tom Evans' feelings concerning the disappointing chart performance of the single also echoed those of his bandmate. From the same 1970 *Magic Christian Music* songbook, he had this to say:

> That period depressed me more than I can say. I hit bottom. I began to think that maybe we weren't really good enough, even with Apple behind us. What I came to realise was that the fault was entirely ours. We sat back. We thought it would just happen. We'd come to Apple and it was the big pop star thing, we didn't need bother, effort.

Around this time, plans for an actual Iveys album began to form and, following a move to Olympic Studios in November, further songs were worked on for the forthcoming album. Late December 1968 saw the band move to another studio, this time to Morgan Studios, with a view to recording a follow-up single to 'Maybe Tomorrow'. With Mal Evans at the production helm this time, the band came up with a song called 'Storm In A Teacup' but this track was ultimately rejected as the next single. The beginning of the new year saw the band return to Trident to continue recording for the new album (with Mal Evans remaining in the producer's chair in place of Tony Visconti). Pleasingly, early 1969 also saw some welcome chart success for the 'Maybe Tomorrow' single in continental Europe. However, this success was not replicated in the US, where the single, released in January, only managed to peak at #67 in the *Billboard* chart.

In between UK touring commitments, the band continued work on the album in the studio. By mid-March, the LP was completed but the band were still in search of a follow-up single to 'Maybe Tomorrow'. They, therefore, returned to the studio in April and worked on a song called 'Give It A Try', but, once again, it was rejected by Apple, which proved incredibly frustrating and disappointing for the band. Unfortunately, the air of despondency hanging over the band's camp was not to improve over the coming months. By mid-1969, Apple was already in a state of internal chaos and American business manager Allen Klein had been brought in to take over the reins of the corporation. This, in turn, led to further problems for the band, for whilst a global release date had initially been set for the new LP, it appeared that Klein had decided to postpone multiple record releases while attempting to resolve the financial chaos at Apple. However, due to the underperformance of the 'Maybe Tomorrow' single in the UK and US, Apple ultimately decided to cancel outright the release of the new album in these markets (although some copies of the LP were actually pressed and distributed in the UK before being pulled). Thankfully, because the single had done well in some other European markets and also Japan, the new LP was still released in these regions (in September 1969). A follow-up single, 'Dear Angie', was also pulled from the new record for release in the territories where the lead single had achieved some success. With things not working out quite as expected with Apple, the band were not surprisingly feeling a tad disappointed at this juncture. Indeed, in the July 1969 edition of *Disc and Music Echo*, the band revealed their feelings at the time – Ron Griffiths:

> We do feel a bit neglected ... We keep writing songs for a new single and submitting them to Apple, but the Beatles keep sending them back saying they're not good enough.

Tom Evans, meanwhile, proffered the following:

> We're going to keep on writing, and we're determined to come up with something the Beatles like. At first, we were adamant about not recording anything but one of our own songs, but now we'd record anything, so long as it was good...

Rather fortuitously, it turned out that a certain Beatle had caught wind of this article and things were about to change for the better...

As for the actual *Maybe Tomorrow* LP, it's, unsurprisingly, a rather mixed bag. Because the band were primarily focused on producing a hit single rather than a LP, the resultant compilation of songs from a variety of recording sessions makes for a hotchpotch of sounds and styles, including rock, pop, psychedelia and even old-time music hall! Whilst comparisons with The Beatles are obvious even at this early stage, they often resemble the early sounds of the Bee Gees too. However, despite lacking a clearly identifiable sound at this point in time, the seeds of something rather special with regards to songwriting can be detected, especially in the likes of the baroque pop of 'Maybe Tomorrow' and the heavy, rifftastic closing number 'I've Been Waiting'. Indeed, despite the mishmash of styles and inconsistent quality, the record still actually makes for a very pleasurable listen and although the overall sound may have been a bit outdated even upon its release (given that The Beatles had just recently delivered the *White Album*), it's still a very likeable album which boasts some terrific vocal prowess from both Pete and Tom and also some deliciously inventive lead guitar playing from Pete. The LP's cover is a tad uninspired, however, featuring just a group photo of all four band members, albeit one which exhibits the fresh-faced innocence and mop-topped smiles of the band at this time. Interestingly, because of the ultimately limited release schedule of the album, copies of the original Japanese and European vinyl pressings became very rare and highly sought-after collectables and even the later 1992 CD reissue (with bonus tracks) became rare due to its limited run (although the album was again reissued on CD in the 2000s in certain territories with the same bonus tracks as the 1992 release – rather strangely, though, this album was not reissued as part of Apple's major reissue programme in 2010 whereas all the other relevant Badfinger titles were).

'See-Saw, Granpa'* (Ham)
The album kicks off in a nice, lively style with this engagingly energetic rocker. Channelling an infectious 1950s rock 'n' roll spirit, this Ham-penned track boasts a swaggeringly upbeat melody performed enthusiastically by the entire band. Pete does an admirable job on lead vocals, but it's Tom's raucous and exuberant backing vocals that are a real highlight. Pete's lead guitar work also impresses throughout, but the tune is truly enhanced by some dazzling piano work courtesy of guest musician Nicky Hopkins. Enthusiastic handclaps pervade the entire track and the overall sense of fun and enjoyment generated by the band on this lead-off track is palpable.

'Beautiful And Blue'* (Evans)
This rather sad ballad, composed by Tom, tells the story of an unhappy and lonely teenage girl suffering from suicidal thoughts. Despite the rather depressing narrative of the song, the melody is really quite beautiful. Rich orchestration and lush vocal harmonies permeate the track and evoke the sound of early Bee Gees. Confident and sensitive lead vocals from Tom help imbue the track with an appropriate sense of melancholia and there is also some very impressive and interesting lead guitar work from Pete throughout. In conclusion, this is a very nice slice of mid-paced pop balladry.

'Dear Angie' (Griffiths)
Written by bassist Ron for his wife, this string-laden ballad exhibits a lovely pleasing lilt and easy-on-the-ear melody. Ron takes on lead vocal duties and handles them with aplomb whilst Pete and Tom supply the exquisitely harmonious backing vocals. This tender, swaying, McCartney-esque ballad was actually released as a follow-up single to 'Maybe Tomorrow' in certain territories (Germany, France, Holland, Sweden: September 1969 and Japan: October 1969) where it was backed with 'No Escaping Your Love'.

'Think About The Good Times' (Gibbins)
Written by drummer Mike Gibbins, this beat-driven little number has shades of mid-1960s Kinks about it. The track exhibits some rather unusual and

distinctive guitar riffing throughout, courtesy of Pete and his wah-wah pedal, but this makes for the true highlight of the track. As for the lead vocals, the song's composer takes ownership on this one and Mike actually makes a pretty decent job of it, ably supported by Tom Evans on backing vox. Short and sweet at just over two minutes in length, it certainly doesn't outstay its welcome.

'Yesterday Ain't Coming Back' (Ham, Evans)
Launching with what sounds like blasts of toy trumpets (allegedly, due to budget constraints, the band had to create a do-it-yourself horn section using that old trusted paper and comb method!), this rather nostalgic sounding number is quite schizophrenic in nature. Aside from the paper and comb horn section, we have some lovely crooning from Pete in the verses disrupted by some rather jarring choruses where the faster and more aggressive tempo of the collective vocals seems to have come from a completely different song. The chorus sections also feature this weird, frog-like, ribbiting bass sound in the background which just adds to the overall absurdity of the track. Having said this, however, the tune is still eminently likeable and possesses a unique charm!

'Fisherman'* (Evans)
Opening up with the sounds of ocean waves rolling upon the beach and seagulls squawking, this acoustic-based, sea shanty-style number features a lovely lilting melody throughout. Tom's lead vocals are pitched perfectly, but it's the catchy chorus with its lush harmonies, evoking the Graham Nash-era Hollies, that provides the real highlight. The lyrics may be guilty of being a little vapid, but I still have a bit of a soft spot for this melodious little tune.

'Maybe Tomorrow' (Evans)
Released as a single A-side (b/w 'And Her Daddy's A Millionaire'): November 1968 (UK), did not chart; January 1969 (US), chart #67
Written by Tom in 1967 about a girl he knew, this beautifully arranged slice of baroque pop is pure class. Quite rightly released as the global lead-off single, it somehow bizarrely failed to catch on at all in the UK and made no impression on the charts whatsoever. Its performance in the US was only marginally better, eventually peaking on the *Billboard* chart at a lowly #67 in March 1969. Fortunately, certain parts of continental Europe (Germany and The Netherlands, in particular) showed more discerning taste and rewarded the track with some appreciable chart success. Quite right, too, for this is a splendidly catchy and melodic tune indeed, replete with gorgeous, soaring vocal harmonies from Tom and Pete (betraying a clear and obvious Everly Brothers influence) and lush, ornate string orchestration. Tony Visconti excels on this track and his immaculate production and arrangement elevate the song into a class of its own. A truly breathtaking, epic pop song which never fails to induce goosebumps in this particular listener – awesome stuff!

An interesting BBC Radio One session version, recorded sometime between February and April 1969, was made available on the bonus audio CD given away with the second edition of Dan Matovina's brilliant book, *Without You: The Tragic Story of Badfinger* (Frances Glover Books, 2000). This BBC session take offers a fairly impressive live reproduction of the song with Pete and Tom playing all the string parts on their guitars.

'Sali Bloo' (Ham)

Founded on a rhythm and blues beat, this Pete Ham composition is a very lively and energetic piece and eminently likeable. Kicking off with a dash of wah-wah infused guitar, Pete gets down to some seriously irresistible and compelling riffing before Ron launches into the vocals. Ron's singing is top-notch and he is ably supported by Pete's backing vocals on this particular tune. Driven along by an insistent up-tempo and pounding beat, this is a terrific little head-rocking and toe-tapping tune.

'Angelique' (Evans)

Another Tom Evans-penned number clearly influenced by the harmonious sounds of the Everly Brothers, this sweet-sounding ballad may be a little too twee for some, but it still has its charms. Tom sings tenderly and earnestly atop a well-arranged musical foundation from which the beautiful tinkling sounds of a harpsichord stand out as a particularly pretty highlight. It all floats along in a pleasingly lilting manner and at only two-and-a-half minutes in length, the saccharine narrative doesn't become overly cloying.

'I'm In Love' (Ham)

A mid-paced, lightweight, yet utterly joyful pop number, it's hard to dislike this perky and happy-sounding little tune. Tom takes on the lead vocal duties, backed up by Pete. The slightly over-the-top spoken voice in the call-and-response section comes courtesy of Pete (well, it was Pete according to producer Tony Visconti in his autobiography. Other sources, however, assert that it was actually Ron who was responsible for the spoken voice part). It's hardly ground-breaking stuff, but it's fun, catchy, and despite sounding decidedly more mid-1960s rather than late-1960s, it's all perfectly innocuous and amiable stuff.

'They're Knocking Down Our Home'* (Ham)

This old school music hall throwback, composed by Pete, is reminiscent of Paul McCartney's more whimsical and nostalgic numbers (such as 'Honey Pie' from the then-recent *White Album*). Pete croons away beautifully against an attractively arranged instrumental backdrop of piano, brass and woodwind. Interestingly, the impressive piano work on this one comes courtesy of the band's manager, Bill Collins, who displays a real flair for tickling the ivories.

It's a particularly effective, nostalgia-laden piece and presents yet another different side to the band, which is very appealing indeed.

An interesting electric guitar demo version of the track was also made available on the bonus CD that accompanied the second edition of Dan Matovina's Badfinger biography.

'I've Been Waiting' (Ham)
In complete contrast to the retro sounds of the preceding track, the album's closing track is the most contemporary. Composed by Pete, this is a heavy dose of jamming and riffing and clearly betrays a Cream-like influence. The elaborate and immaculate production and arrangement found elsewhere on the LP is done away with and the band are let loose to express themselves musically. Pete's searing lead guitar riffing impresses throughout whilst ably supported by Mike's pounding drums and Ron's sublime bass work. Pete's lead vocals are also terrific and the collective harmonious vocal sounds throughout are utterly spellbinding. At five minutes in length, this is an epic conclusion to the album – heavy, psychedelic, enthralling – and it's no surprise that this standout track is a real fan favourite.

Other Contemporary Songs
'No Escaping Your Love' (Evans)
The B-side to the 'Dear Angie' single, this track dates from the band's earliest recording session for Apple. Lightweight, perky and poppy, it's definitely more 1964 than 1968/9 in feel. However, it's catchy enough and perfectly likeable, if all a little bit throwaway. Tom's lead vocal is engaging and the backing vocals are nice and harmonious as you'd expect. So, overall, it's a good, harmless, fun pop song! This track was released as a bonus track on the 1992 CD reissue of the album.

'Mrs Jones' (Ham)
Featuring a strong, assured lead vocal from Pete, this catchy and buoyant pop tune again originates from the earliest Apple recording sessions. As with the previous track, this too sounds a tad dated, exuding a more mid-1960s feel than late-1960s – indeed, the high-pitched backing vox resemble those found on The Beatles' 'Paperback Writer' – but it still makes for a truly captivating listen. This previously unreleased track was also released as a bonus track on the 1992 CD reissue.

'And Her Daddy's A Millionaire' (Ham, Evans)
The B-side to 'Maybe Tomorrow', this tune once again stems from those earliest Apple recording sessions in July 1968. However, the version that appeared on the single was actually a later re-recording of the song from the following month. Boasting a catchy and infectious rock riff, this lively and

upbeat pop tune positively bristles with energy. Tom delivers a fairly frenetic lead vocal over the urgent beat, which is definitely at the rockier sounding end of the pop spectrum. At a smidge over two minutes in length, it's a short and sweet blast of good-time guitar pop. This track was also released as a bonus track on the 1992 CD reissue.

'Looking For My Baby' (Ham)
Dating from a Spring 1968 (pre-Apple) recording session, this track was actually self-produced by The Iveys. It's another fun and lightweight pop song, albeit a tad throwaway, and actually resembles some of David Bowie's mid-1960s 'vaudeville' pop with its slightly silly sounding vocal effects. Another tune that barely breaks through the two-minute duration barrier, it's fairly inconsequential stuff, but it does provide an interesting musical insight into the early stage of the band. This previously unreleased track was also released as a bonus track on the 1992 CD reissue.

'Permissive Paradise' (Cox, Sidey)
Now this one's a real oddity! Recorded by The Iveys under the pseudonym The Pleasure Garden, this track was recorded (probably around April/May 1969) for a flexidisc promoting a photo book called *Young London* (documenting Swinging London in the 1960s). Given how obscure this disc was (and the fact that the band recorded under a pseudonym), this track was ultimately never associated with the band and it wasn't until 2002 (33 years after the recording!) that it was rediscovered by some fans and correctly reinserted into the band's discography. The songwriting is credited to Jeremy Cox and John Sidey, but these could well be a pseudonym for Gilles Cremonesi, an employee of the book's publishing company.

As for the song itself, it's okay, but it's definitely no lost classic. The archetypal mid-1960s sound is reminiscent of several tracks on the *Maybe Tomorrow* album, but the song does possess a reasonably catchy guitar riff in addition to some enthusiastic band vocals (Ron Griffiths impressively handles the lead vocal duties on this one with backing from Tom and Pete). This song is available on at least two different CDs: *Syde Tryps One* (Wooden Hill, 1995) and *The Best Of The Rubble Collection, Vol. 3* (Bam-Caruso Records, 1999).

'Catherine Cares' (Ham)
Written in 1968 by Pete Ham as an ode to his mum, this charming slice of catchy guitar pop was probably not under any serious consideration for release by the band (as it was simply intended as a heartfelt 'thank you' gift to his mother) but it's still a great little tune and, by all accounts, his mum was absolutely thrilled with the song! This demo track is available on Pete Ham's first CD collection of home demos, *7 Park Avenue* (Rykodisc, 1997).

'Weep Baby' (Ham)
An acoustic ballad written for his girlfriend of the time, this Pete Ham-penned demo song is emotionally intimate and delicately performed. This one dates from around late-1967. This home demo is also available on Pete's 7 *Park Avenue* CD.

'Island' (Ham)
Another Pete Ham home demo, this one dates from around 1968. On this track, Pete masterfully evokes the image of a tropical island paradise with his Hawaiian-sounding slide guitar licks. The whole song effectively exudes an air of serenity and tranquillity with its beautiful, laid-back and lilting melody. This demo is again available on Pete's 7 *Park Avenue* CD.

'Makes Me Feel Good' (Ham)
This Pete Ham demo song originates from 1967 and serves up a wonderful two minutes of embryonic power-pop. Boasting a glorious melody, this charming and upbeat pop number is full of lovely chord changes that provide ample evidence of Pete's strength as a songwriter, even at this early stage. Two different versions of this home demo are available on Pete's *Golders Green* CD, his second collection of home demos (Rykodisc, 1999) – one dating from 1967, the other from 1968.

'I'll Kiss You Goodnight' (Ham)
Originating from around 1966/1967, this Pete Ham song reflects his more tender, romantic side. An extremely moving and sweet-sounding ballad, the melody is incredibly strong whilst the emotional maturity of the lyrics also impresses given how young Pete was when he wrote this one. This definitely stands as another fine early example of Pete's songwriting ability. The rest of his bandmates obviously liked this one too, as The Iveys as a whole worked on this track in the studio during the latter half of 1967. The Pete Ham home demo version can also be found on Pete's *Golders Green* CD.

Note: The Iveys cut numerous demos around 1967-1968 (at their home studio in 7 Park Avenue, Golders Green, London) and eleven of these previously unreleased tracks were released during the 2000s on Apple-focused various artists' CD compilations (issued by the RPM label): *94 Baker Street: The Pop-Psych Sounds Of The Apple Era 1967-1969* (2003), *An Apple A Day: More Pop-Psych Sounds From The Apple Era 1967-1969* (2006) and *Treacle Toffee World: Further Adventures Into The Pop-Psych Sounds From The Apple Era 1967-1969* (2008). The songs which appear across these three compilations include:

'I'm Too Shy' (Evans)
An infectiously catchy pop tune whose highlights include a thunderous skin-pounding demonstration from Mike Gibbins and some wonderful, harmonious vocal 'Ahhhh's throughout the song. This commercial-sounding track stands as

another fine example of Tom's prolific and high-quality songwriting from this early period.

'Maybe Tomorrow' (Evans)
An embryonic version of the classic debut single. Fundamentally, not that much different from the finalised version – this demo version merely lacks the ornate string orchestration and Tony Visconti's production finesse.

'Tube Train' (Griffiths)
Penned by Ron, this very literal ode to the tube train, replete with authentic-sounding audio effects, exhibits a slighter tougher veneer with its early Who-like vibe.

'She Came Out Of The Cold' (Evans, Ham)
A melancholic, ghost story played out over a super, pixiphone-enhanced melody results in an impressive display of mature songwriting ability from Tom and Pete at this early stage. An alternative version of this track was also made available on the bonus CD that accompanied the second edition of the Dan Matovina-authored Badfinger biography (*Without You: The Tragic Story of Badfinger* - Frances Glover Books, 2000).

'I've Been There Once Before' (Ham)
This song details a premonition that Pete had concerning an air show plane collision. This cheery tale features a superb lead vocal from Pete and, again, some thundering drumming from Mike. The track climaxes impressively with a tremendous instrumental cacophony that simulates the sound of the falling planes.

'Black & White Rainbows' (Ham)
This fairly catchy number was apparently recorded before Tom Evans joined the band and therefore features rhythm guitarist Dai Jenkins instead. This melodic and vocally harmonious number evokes a more Mod-ish feel again and also benefits from some nice wah-wah guitar work, courtesy of Pete Ham.

'Girl Next Door In The Miniskirt' (Ham)
The title says it all, really. This is Pete's poppy ode to the girl next door in the miniskirt! Not exactly Pete's finest musical moment, lyrically and structurally, this one is a bit of a mess! This track is also actually mistitled on the *An Apple A Day* CD as 'Girl In A Mini Skirt'.

'Tomorrow's Today' (Evans)
Featuring jangly, psych-tinged guitars, this tune boasts a fairly intricate melody and is sung by Tom with assistance from Ron. Again, this was mistitled on the *An Apple A Day* CD as 'Tomorrow Today'.

'Mr Strangeways' (Griffiths)

A quirky, psych-pop oddity from the pen of Ron Griffiths, this is exuberant fun but the melody's all over the place! It's a humorous piece and, ultimately, a bit of a Mod-ish musical curio which again exhibits an early Who-like vibe.

'Bittersweet Adieu' (Griffiths)

Another Ron Griffiths-penned composition, this one boasts a terrifically moody-sounding melody. An autobiographical song about the band's life on the road, it features a very impressive lead vocal from Ron and shines a light on the songwriting talent of the Iveys' bassist.

'How Does It Feel' (Evans)

This is a fairly by-the-numbers poppy love song. It's effervescent, lightweight, fun, but utterly disposable froth nonetheless! Tom handles lead vocal duties on this one and is ably backed by Ron and Pete.

Further Iveys demos were also made available on the respective bonus CDs that accompanied both editions of the Matovina-authored Badfinger biography:

'Good Times Together' (Evans)

This is Tom's first recorded solo demo after joining The Iveys in August 1967. Tom plays electric guitar and double tracks his own voice on this Everly Brothers inspired number. It's a sweet-sounding tune, very quaint, but ultimately sounds very outdated for 1967. This track was made available on the bonus CD given away with the first edition of *Without You: The Tragic Story of Badfinger* (Frances Glover Books, 1997).

'Take Good Care Of My Baby' (Ham)

This early-1968 Iveys demo, penned by Pete, was one of the demo songs submitted to various record companies at the time, including Apple. A mid-tempo pop number, it's an okay song, if a little inconsequential. However, the track is elevated somewhat by some superlative lead guitar and vocals courtesy of the song's composer. This track was made available on the bonus CD that accompanied the second edition of Matovina's book (Frances Glover Books, 2000).

'Clown Of The Party' (Ham)

Another Ham-penned Iveys demo, this one kicks off with a terrific blast of fairly heavy sounding, distorted lead guitar from Pete before it settles down somewhat into a pleasant enough ditty about a sad clown. The backing vocals are pleasingly enthusiastic and Ron also plays a great bass part too. This likeable track is also available on the bonus CD that came with the second edition of the Matovina tome.

'Taxi' (Ham)

Composed by Pete but sung by Ron Griffiths, this simple love song is all about a couple taking a taxi ride to the girlfriend's home. This demo was actually one of the demos produced by Ray Davies back in January 1967 (and features Dai Jenkins in the band's line-up). It's fairly typical sounding mid-1960s pop fare, perfectly listenable but ultimately unremarkable. This demo track was also made available on the bonus CD given away with the second edition of the Matovina book.

Magic Christian Music

Personnel:
Pete Ham: vocals, guitars, keyboards
Tom Evans: vocals, rhythm/bass guitars
Ron Griffiths: vocals, bass guitar
Mike Gibbins: vocals, drums
Recorded at Trident, Abbey Road and IBC Studios, London, UK (April – November 1969, new recordings only)
Produced by Tony Visconti, Mal Evans* and Paul McCartney**
UK release date: January 1970
US release date: February 1970
Highest chart places: UK: Did not chart, US: 55

In late July 1969, Paul McCartney set up a meeting with The Iveys. Having read about their grievances and their feeling of 'neglect' in the recent *Disc and Music Echo* article, he wanted to talk about an upcoming project with them that he hoped would resolve the situation. Paul had been asked to contribute some songs to an upcoming film project, entitled *The Magic Christian* (a satirical, black comedy which would feature his bandmate, Ringo Starr, starring opposite Peter Sellers), but he wasn't that keen on doing it, given that he was extremely busy with other projects (including the completion of the Beatles' *Abbey Road* album). Therefore, he decided to offer the gig to The Iveys. A few days prior to his meeting with the band, McCartney had recorded a demo of a song he had in mind for the movie and which he thought could be a hit single – the song was called 'Come And Get It'.

At the meeting, he played the band his demo and, famously, informed them that if they recorded this song exactly as he'd demoed it, they'd end up with a sure-fire hit on their hands. Also, if they did a good job on this song, then they'd also have the opportunity to record some other songs for the movie. The band reportedly had slightly mixed feelings about all this – on the one hand, they weren't keen on covering other people's songs and felt that they should be concentrating on recording their own material, but on the other hand, this was also a fantastic opportunity to work with the one and only Paul McCartney and it was somewhat flattering that he considered them worthy enough to record one of his songs. Therefore, any concerns soon dissipated, and the band readily accepted Paul's offer. The band entered Abbey Road Studios at the beginning of August 1969 and cut 'Come And Get It' with McCartney producing the track. The end result was a resounding success, so much so that McCartney felt confident enough to let the band record another couple of tracks for the forthcoming movie. So, by the end of the month, they were back in the studio to start working on the new tracks with McCartney still at the production helm.

During September, bassist Ron Griffiths fell seriously ill with chickenpox and was unable to attend any further recording sessions. Unfortunately, this illness occurred at a time when Ron's relationship with the rest of the band was already becoming increasingly strained. He was now, by this time, a responsible, married man with a child in tow, which didn't exactly sit too well with the rock 'n' roll lifestyle. He had therefore been drifting apart from his bandmates anyway but his recent illness was the final nail in the coffin. By mutual agreement (if somewhat begrudgingly on Ron's side), he left the band and took on the more secure and reliable role of a factory worker. However, with the 'Come And Get It' single due out in December and an accompanying album now scheduled (it had been decided by the Apple powers that be that it would be a good idea to cash in on the extensive media coverage and publicity generated by *The Magic Christian* movie by rush-releasing a new band album), they now needed to promptly recruit a replacement for Ron.

However, before that and amidst all these new developments, it was also agreed, by all relevant parties, that this was now the perfect moment for a change of band moniker. Feeling that 'The Iveys' sounded a tad dated at this juncture, and fed up of getting mixed up with another British band called The Ivy League, the band and their associates set about coming up with a suitable new name. Potential names bandied about included 'Home' (a Paul McCartney idea) and the rather cheekier 'Prix' (suggested by John Lennon). In the end, Apple Corps' Neil Aspinall reportedly came up with the suggestion of 'Badfinger', inspired by 'Bad Finger Boogie', an early working title of the Beatles' 'With A Little Help From My Friends' – apparently, Lennon had been playing the piano with an injured finger and labelled the musical piece accordingly!

To tie in with the forthcoming movie, it was decided that the new album would be entitled *Magic Christian Music*. However, due to a lack of new material and a fast-approaching release date, it was also decided to bolster the track listing with old Iveys tracks. Both Mal Evans and Paul McCartney got involved with this process and several old tracks were duly dusted off and given the remix treatment.

Just prior to the UK release of the 'Come And Get It' single in December 1969, the newly-christened Badfinger found their new member. Liverpool-born Joey Molland (21 June 1947) was a real find – charismatic, good-looking, enthusiastic and a highly talented guitarist – he was a perfect fit for the band. Although he was only in his early 20s at the time, he was already a veteran musician and had most recently spent time playing with Gary Walker and The Rain, who had enjoyed some success in Japan. The introduction of Joey, a rhythm and lead guitarist, did also result in Tom Evans switching to bass guitar, but this slight shuffling of roles aside, the new line-up was ready to go. However, before Joey had even had a proper chance to catch his breath, things just exploded.

The new single crashed into the UK charts (eventually peaking at #4), the movie premiered (and whilst the movie received rather mixed reviews, the music was universally lauded) and the new LP made its UK appearance in January 1970. That January also saw the global release of the 'Come And Get It' single, where the UK chart success was replicated in pretty much every other territory (in the US, the single peaked at #7 in the *Billboard* Hot 100). Badfinger suddenly found themselves in great demand. A UK tour was undertaken during the early months of the new year and there was also a flurry of European TV appearances, including a performance on the prestigious *Top of the Pops*. The new LP was released in the US in February, where it eventually peaked at #55 in the *Billboard* 200 (interestingly, the US version dropped two songs from the track listing – 'Angelique' and 'Give It A Try'). Given all this success, it was then strange that no further singles were lifted from the record.

Regarding reviews of the new LP published at the time, they were generally pretty positive across the board. *Record Mirror*: 'Rather a good pop LP ... their own songs are as strong as Paul McCartney's pleasing 'Come And Get It'.' *Cash Box*: '...the LP is rich with a sound much like the Beatles' last two albums ... Badfinger has turned out intelligent and melodic rock...' Most other reviews continued in this positive vein, with pretty much all of them also making the same inevitable comparisons with The Beatles.

My take on the album is similar to my opinion of the *Maybe Tomorrow* LP in that, due to its patchwork nature, it doesn't quite hold together as an entirely cohesive collection of songs. Listeners at the time were probably left reeling somewhat from the bombardment of differing musical styles, genres and influences – baroque pop, psychedelia, rock, folk – but on the positive side, the wide variety of ideas on display does show off their incredibly broad musical palette and there's little chance of getting bored whilst listening to it – there's something for everybody on this LP! The newer songs continue to highlight a burgeoning songwriting talent whilst the vocals and musicianship also continue to impress. So, at this point in time, they still lacked a clearly identifiable musical identity, but with a new band moniker and re-jigged line-up now firmly in place, that would change on the next album. Interestingly, Pete Ham also shared his rather illuminating and astute thoughts on the band at this juncture when interviewed for the accompanying *Magic Christian Music* songbook (1970):

To be quite honest, I think we conned our way into Apple at first. We didn't deserve it; we weren't that good. I think the fact that we wrote good songs saved us, and we've also tried to justify being here by trying to get ourselves together, I think we're worth it now. The songs we do are usually very varied, but I'm thinking we'd better start trying to put them into one category. People in this business like to put other people into a bag. You can branch out when you've got established, but I reckon our early mistake was being too varied too soon.

As for the LP cover, it was designed by David King and was clearly influenced by the likes of Giorgio de Chirico and René Magritte. The front image depicts a large hand with its index finger pointing skyward, with a nail piercing the finger. The surreal back cover features head shots of Pete, Tom and Mike only. The fact that only three band members were shown must have added to the overall confusion (to consumers) generated by the cover information. The sleeve notes (courtesy of Mal Evans) mention Joey as a band member yet Joey, of course, never played a note on the LP and his photo is nowhere to be seen (presumably, the cover artwork had all been finalised prior to Joey joining). However, Ron's name also appears on the record as one of the songwriters even though he'd left the band by this time, so of course there was no photo of him either. All of this must have caused a few listeners to scratch their heads in confusion as to who was actually in the band's line-up at that time! Also, interestingly, Paul McCartney chose not to take any production credits on the original LP, so the original production credits are shared out between Tony Visconti (who produced some of the old Iveys numbers) and Mal Evans. This has gradually, although less than perfectly, been rectified on subsequent CD reissues (the album was first released on CD in 1991, with a couple of added bonus tracks, and reissued again in 2010 in CD and digital formats as part of Apple's major reissue campaign, with various bonus tracks spread across both formats).

As for *The Magic Christian* official soundtrack album, this was released in February 1970 in the US (on the Commonwealth United Records label) and in April 1970 in the UK (on the Pye record label). Aside from the three Badfinger songs ('Come And Get It', 'Carry On Till Tomorrow' and 'Rock Of All Ages'), the rest of the soundtrack is mainly made up of incidental music (scored by Ken Thorne, who had also scored the music for the Beatles' *Help!* movie) and the Thunderclap Newman song, 'Something In The Air'.

'Come And Get It'** (McCartney)
Released as a single A-side (b/w 'Rock Of All Ages'): December 1969 (UK), chart #4; January 1970 (US), chart #7
Under the tutelage of Paul McCartney in the studio, the band reproduced his original demo version of the song near perfectly, the only real noticeable difference being the slightly faster tempo of their version. The end result is a perfectly formed little pop-rocker. Primarily a piano-based number, the melody is also significantly driven along by an incredibly solid and well-defined drum beat from Mike and enthusiastic percussion (some of which was actually played by McCartney). Regarding the lead vocals, Paul apparently auditioned all four members to see whose voice would suit the song best and ultimately determined that it would be Tom who took that honour. This turned out to be a great decision as Tom absolutely nails the vocals with a perfectly pitched performance. The rest of the boys in the band get to add their sumptuous backing harmonies throughout, all ideally balanced in the mix so as not to overshadow Tom's lead voice.

Short and sweet, at just under two and a half minutes in length, this terrifically catchy pop tune quite rightly became a global smash hit and given its obvious Beatles-y sound, it's no wonder that a lot of first-time listeners mistook it for a new tune by the Fab Four! As for how the band felt working with the Beatle legend, Pete Ham summed it up nicely in the *Magic Christian Music* songbook (1970):

> I found working with Paul McCartney on 'Come And Get It' a fantastic experience. He really brought it out of us, showed us what it should be like. Very relaxed.

Note: You can find Paul McCartney's original demo version of the song on both The Beatles' *Anthology 3* (Apple, 1996) and the super deluxe 50th anniversary edition of *Abbey Road* (Apple, 2019).

'Crimson Ship'** (Evans, Ham, Gibbins)

Boasting another primarily piano-based melody, this tasty, post-psych tune was written as a doff of the hat to McCartney and his support of the band. Most of the lyrics reportedly came from Tom and they reference their recent work with the Beatle, albeit rather obliquely at times. However, the first verse seems fairly clear:

> My life was coloured, painting pictures out of tune
> He came from nowhere in a song
> It might have been the way I laughed, he made the jokes
> Could only show me what was wrong

The dual lead vocals from Tom and Pete are a delight, with Pete's rich, tenor voice and Tom's higher-pitched vocals complementing each other perfectly. Due to Ron Griffiths' absence from the recording sessions through illness, Tom also takes over the bass duties for this one and does an impeccable job. Pete contributes some distinctively tasty lead guitar throughout as well, which adds real character to the piece. The song's incredibly strong hook inveigles its way into the listener's head and the end result is a pleasingly memorable effort.

'Dear Angie' (Griffiths)

Lifted from the previous *Maybe Tomorrow* LP, this remixed version of the track holds no further surprises for the listener.

'Fisherman'* (Evans)

Another track lifted from the previous album to make up the numbers, the obvious amendment in this remix is the removal of most of the sound effects employed in the original version. This would probably have pleased certain listeners who weren't all that keen on the 'novelty song' vibe of the original. One other minor change saw the final chorus being cut.

'Midnight Sun'* (Ham)

This Pete Ham composition gives an indication of where the band were headed musically. Rockier than most of their previous output and certainly more contemporary sounding, this extremely catchy rock 'n' roll tune features some sizzling lead guitar licks from Pete. The rest of the band offer equally enthusiastic instrumental backing, with Tom handling bass duties again. Pete's lead vocals are strong and confident and he is ably backed up by Tom in the background. This riff-filled rocker exudes a lot of charm and makes for a fine addition to the album.

An energetic and engaging live performance of the song was captured from BBC Radio's *Jimmy Saville Speakeasy Radio Show*, broadcast on 20 February 1970, and was made available on the bonus audio CD that accompanied the second edition of the Matovina-authored band biography.

'Beautiful And Blue'* (Evans)

Another old Iveys track retrieved and dusted off for the new record. The remix offers nothing more than a polished-up sound.

'Rock Of All Ages'** (Evans, Gibbins, Ham)

This superb rocker, again produced by McCartney, is a real gem. As with 'Midnight Sun', this shows the band starting to display a much harder edge to their music. It's a rollicking, good-time rock number featuring an absolutely throat-shredding vocal performance from Tom (reminiscent of the McCartney 'rock' voice on tracks such as 'Long Tall Sally', 'I'm Down' and 'Helter Skelter'). Bursting with energy, this incredibly infectious number also benefits from the keyboard skills of their Beatle mentor, who does his best Jerry Lee Lewis impression on this one. Tom again plays bass on this for the absent Ron, whilst the searing lead guitar throughout from Pete is stunning.

Firing on all cylinders for the entire duration of the song, the band throw everything into this and listeners are rewarded with a breathlessly exciting rock song. Interestingly, the song also contains some rather prophetic lyrics which would come back to haunt the band in the not-too-distant future: 'You're taking all my money and I guess you think it's funny, but I don't'.

'Carry On Till Tomorrow'** (Evans, Ham)

This Pete and Tom co-writing effort is a real highlight of the album. Intentionally evoking the spirit of Simon and Garfunkel, this haunting folk-style number opens quietly with some chiming acoustic finger picking before Tom's gentle, angelic voice enters the picture. The song then continues to build, slowly but surely, with the introduction of some beautifully scored strings carrying the tune to a mid-song crescendo where Pete's blistering lead guitar solo takes centre stage. The song then retreats back to its original serene setting for one more verse and chorus before once again taking flight towards the end with soaring orchestration and scintillating lead guitar. The song's choral coda, with its exquisite blend of ethereal vocal harmonies, provides a fitting climax to this beautiful and heart-rending ballad.

This magnificently moody and atmospheric number oozes class and this is due in no small part to the presence of the fifth Beatle himself, George Martin, on this track, as he was responsible for scoring the strings. This is, quite simply, a spine-tingling moment on the album.

An acoustic-based demo version of the song featuring Tom and Pete was also made available on the bonus CD that accompanied the first edition of the Dan Matovina tome.

'I'm In Love'* (Ham)

Another old Iveys track selected to pad out the album's track listing, this one actually had the vocals redone and re-recorded. The call-and-response section was also omitted this time around.

'Walk Out In The Rain'* (Ham)

This gentle and sensitive ballad from the pen of Pete Ham delivers the album's most heart-breaking moment. Incredibly graceful and tender, this exquisite tune features Pete in fine vocal form. His sweet-sounding and sensitive delivery of the melancholic lyrics adds a real poignancy to the proceedings and admirably demonstrates Pete's ability to compose songs that readily tug at listeners' heartstrings. During the second half of the song, Tom's secondary vocals appear as he effectively shadows Pete's lead, resulting in a very pleasing vocal sound reminiscent of the Everly Brothers or, indeed, the early Beatles. Towards the end of the song, Pete attempts to join Tom in the higher vocal register as he goes all falsetto on us and we're left gasping in wonderment at the angelic choral fade-out.

'Angelique' (Evans)

Another old track lifted from *Maybe Tomorrow*, this one loses its original horn flourishes in the remix. Otherwise, it's pretty much the same as before.

'Knocking Down Our Home'* (Ham)

Yet another remixed older track, this one has no real discernible differences from the original version aside from a slightly improved sound.

'Give It A Try'* (Evans, Gibbins, Ham, Griffiths)

Originally conceived in the studio as a possible follow-up single to 'Maybe Tomorrow', all four band members contributed to this number. In a desperate attempt to come up with a hit single, they pretty much throw everything at this one. It's perky and cheerful guitar pop with a distinct mid-1960s feel replete with sickly sweet 'weee-oooo' backing vocals. Whilst it is essentially harmless, bubble-gum fun featuring forgettable generic lyrics about love and the like, it remains pretty disposable stuff really and, in all honesty, does end up sounding a tad contrived. It isn't surprising that Apple rejected this as a follow-up single. For me, the most exciting part of the song comes near the end with a brief blast of proto-Glam guitar work that actually brings to mind David Bowie's 'Starman'!

'Maybe Tomorrow' (Evans)

Again, another song lifted from the previous Iveys album. The sound has been improved in the remix, but no major detectable changes otherwise.

Other Contemporary Songs
'Storm In A Teacup'* (Evans)

This was the band's first deliberate attempt at coming up with a follow-up single to 'Maybe Tomorrow'. Recorded late in December 1968, Mal Evans sat in the producer's chair for this one. Ultimately, this track was rejected by Apple as a single, but it did actually end up appearing on a special promotional EP released in collaboration with Wall's Ice Cream in July 1969, that was intended to expose various Apple artists to the general public (the other Apple artists on the EP were James Taylor, Jackie Lomax and Mary Hopkin). However, the EP was only available through mail-order, so I'm not sure how much exposure was actually achieved.

As for the song itself, it's an upbeat, catchy pop number featuring some enthusiastic and infectious lead vocal work from Tom and an interesting guitar solo mid-song courtesy of Pete. Overall, there's a bit of a Small Faces vibe about this track, which is no bad thing, and whilst this tune fares better than 'Give It A Try', there's still a sense of contrivance about the whole thing. I think the other problem with both this track and the subsequent 'single' attempt, 'Give It A Try', is that by 1969 they both already sounded two or three years out of date and this may have been another reason why Apple rejected them as follow-up singles.

This song was released as a bonus track on both the 1991 CD album reissue and the 2010 digital album reissue (different mixes, respectively).

'Arthur'* (Evans)

Recorded at the same time as 'Give It A Try' with a view to it being the B-side, this is a fun, upbeat number that sounds like a Kinks/Hollies mash-up. Tom delivers another great lead vocal performance atop what is essentially a keyboard-driven piece. It suffers the same problem as its proposed A-side in that it all sounds more mid-1960s than 1969, but it still remains a charmingly addictive little tune which I actually prefer over both 'Storm In A Teacup' and 'Give It A Try'.

This song was also released as a bonus track on both the 1991 CD album reissue and the 2010 digital reissue (different mixes again, respectively).

'Dawn' (Ham)
This 1969 home demo from Pete ably demonstrates his skill at crafting memorable pop melodies. Poignant and heartfelt, this beautifully strummed piece reflects Pete's more contemplative side. This demo is available on Pete's *Golders Green* CD.

'Evening Sky' (Ham)
Another 1969 home demo by Pete. This is a beautifully haunting and melancholic-sounding piano ballad. This particular demo is available as a bonus track on the Japanese release of Pete's *Golders Green* CD.

Note: Apple's 2010 reissue of *Magic Christian Music* contained additional bonus tracks spread across both the CD and digital formats, but these were just different versions/mixes of *Maybe Tomorrow*-era tracks.
CD: 'And Her Daddy's A Millionaire' (alternative version), 'Mrs. Jones' (remix), 'Sali Bloo' (mono mix), 'See-Saw Granpa' (mono mix), 'I've Been Waiting' (unedited remix)
Digital: 'Dear Angie' (mono mix), 'Think About The Good Times' (mono mix), 'No Escaping Your Love' (mono mix), 'Yesterday Ain't Coming Back' (mono mix)

No Dice

Personnel:
Pete Ham: vocals, guitar, piano
Tom Evans: vocals, bass
Joey Molland: vocals, guitar
Mike Gibbins: vocals, drums
Recorded at Abbey Road and Trident Studios, London, UK (April – August 1970)
Produced by Geoff Emerick and *Mal Evans
Release date: November 1970
Highest chart places: UK: Did not chart, US: 28

In April 1970, the band entered the recording studio for their first session with new recruit Joey Molland. Several numbers were worked on at this initial session with Mal Evans on production duties. By all accounts, this initial session was a little rough around the edges as the new (and reshuffled) line-up attempted to achieve musical harmony in the studio. It was also around this time that manager Bill Collins flew over to the US to scout out the possibility of a tour over there for later in the year. It was at this juncture that a major character in the Badfinger story made his first appearance. US-born Stan Polley, a music business manager, initially became involved with the band to help set up this US tour, but by the end of the year, he had become the band's official business manager and, as we shall discover later, things would never be the same again.

From May through to August of 1970, it was back to the recording studios (Trident and Abbey Road, respectively) for the boys as they continued working on their next LP. Initially, Mal Evans produced the sessions, but by late June, he had been replaced by former Beatles sound engineer Geoff Emerick. Allegedly, Bill Collins had been the primary driving force behind the ousting of Mal as he was apparently paranoid about Mal wanting to take over his Badfinger management role (although in the 2010 CD reissue liner notes, Geoff Emerick states that it was Allen Klein who wanted him to produce the record). Whatever the internal politics regarding Mal, Geoff Emerick was delighted to take over the project as he had been looking to become a producer and this presented him with the perfect opportunity. Around this time, the Badfinger boys also got involved in recording sessions for George Harrison's *All Things Must Pass* LP with Tom, Pete and Joey playing acoustic guitars and Mike helping out on percussion.

In August 1970, the new, completed album was submitted to Apple and it was also decided that the first single from the record would be the track, 'No Matter What'. Interestingly, this song had been one of the first ones worked on with Mal Evans and had already been proposed as a possible single by the band, only to be met with initial rejection by Apple. However, a rethink by the powers that be and a little buffing up courtesy of Geoff Emerick, and the new single was good to go. To accompany the single, a promotional film was shot at a farm in Wales (where the band were rehearsing for the forthcoming US tour) featuring clips of the boys lip-syncing in a barn and walking around the Welsh countryside.

The US tour commenced in September and the setlist focused on material from the new LP together with a few older numbers and cover versions thrown into the mix (the cover versions paid tribute to the likes of Steve Miller and Dave Mason). Whilst on tour, the 'No Matter What' single was first released in the US and then the following month in the UK. The parent album was released globally in November with an eye-catching cover design featuring a scantily clad, Middle Eastern-style female dancer (designed by Apple staff members Richard DiLello and Gene Mahon – incidentally, Gene had previously worked on the *Sgt Pepper* LP cover and the Apple record label design; DiLello is also credited with coming up with the *No Dice* title). The music press reviews of the new album were extremely positive, even if the majority of them persisted in making constant comparisons to The Beatles, which, unsurprisingly, soon began to annoy the band members (but at least they were positive comparisons full of praise and, to be fair, the comparisons were not without validity). Some typical reviews were as follows – *Billboard*:

Badfinger carries on the rhythm-happy tradition of the early Beatles, rocking to the big beat without hang-ups or pretensions of profundity. Pete Ham and Joey Molland write most of the group's original material, but songs, as well as the Liverpool-type voices, cover the Beatles like a Xerox. The catch is they're good, and prove it nicely on 'No Matter What', 'Better Days', 'Without You' and 'I Can't Take It'.

Rolling Stone echoed these sentiments:

With their new album *No Dice*, Badfinger has to their credit one of the best records of the year. This album is literally a quantum jump over their uneven debut album *Magic Christian Music,* and Badfinger is certainly on the way to fulfilling their enormous promise ... the types of songs Badfinger excelled on before are here once again: great rockers and gorgeously done pop rock and roll. The difference is that, this time around, everything else is good as well: the whole album flows well, Pete Ham sings in his best McCartney-esque voice, their guitarist now plays like Eric Clapton, and the material is all very good: the whole album adds up to as close to the monster Badfinger may well make, in time ... in general, this album sounds nothing so much as what might have happened had the post-Pepper Beatles gotten it together after their promising double *The Beatles*. Badfinger is becoming that good, and they may well get better.

Disc and Music Echo, meanwhile, made the following observations:

Badfinger are one of Apple's natural phenomena who continue to disturbingly sound like the early Beatles. I say 'disturbingly' only because the comparison is almost indecent and it becomes harder and harder each time I hear them as a separate Badfinger entity. Still, if you accidentally manage to sound like the Beatles, it can't be bad, and on this album, Badfinger have extended and charged up their lead guitar and rhythm work, so they sound a lot stronger overall than they did on their early album.

Creem were similarly enthused:

...the *No Dice* album sounds like what the Beatles might have done had they gotten it all together after their white album ... However, in songwriting and singing, Badfinger shuts down the post-*Pepper* Beatles cold, and that, I feel, is something most comparisons of the groups sneakily evade talking about ... When Badfinger gets around to making the record they're capable of making, it may be as good as everything the Beatles ever did after *Rubber Soul*, all rolled into one. In the meantime, *No Dice* is merely great.

However, in a January 1971 interview with Chris Charlesworth (for *Melody Maker*), Pete Ham could barely conceal his frustrations with the constant Beatle comparisons:

Everyone who interviews us wants to talk about The Beatles. Sure, we were influenced by the Beatles, like ten million other groups. There are a million groups copying Led Zeppelin at the moment, but nobody bothers to criticise them for it. We like melodies and songs and we get called a second Beatles.

In the same interview, however, Joey Molland did begrudgingly concede that:

The Beatles have done us a lot of good. To have been associated with them has done us a lot of good because they are great people.

Thankfully, the commercial reaction to the LP echoed the positive critical reaction and both the single and album proved incredibly successful. The single peaked at #8 in the US and #5 in the UK, whilst the album peaked at #28 in the US. However, in the UK, the LP only saw moderate sales, but this was probably down to poor domestic promotion due to internal strife at Apple, and the UK perception of the group as a 'singles' band rather than as an 'album' band. In fact, the band clearly expressed their thoughts on the domestic situation in their 1971 *Melody Maker* interview with Chris Charlesworth, as can be seen from the following excerpt:

'What we would really love is to be accepted in this country but it doesn't seem as though we are yet,' said Tom. 'We're not complaining, but it's a fight for us in England,' added Joey. 'English people think of us as the group that did 'Come And Get It'. Full stop,' said Pete. 'They don't seem prepared to listen to other things we do, but in America, they view every number separately'.

The US tour had also gone down well and, after the tour had finished (mid-December), the band met up with Stan Polley to discuss his becoming their permanent, full-time business manager. With promises that they'd all end up as millionaires ringing in their ears, the band signed with Polley in a deal that saw him set to receive 30% gross of all Badfinger income (usually, at that time, 5-10% for a business manager was the usual rate!). One of Polley's first actions, in early 1971, was to set up Badfinger Enterprises Inc. (BEI), a company created in order to hold and manage all of the band's income. With Polley in charge of the funds and him owning the majority of stock in this new endeavour, alarm bells should already have started ringing. However, the beguiled band were currently riding the crest of a wave with their recent success and saw no reason at this point in time to doubt Stan the man – this viewpoint would change dramatically over the coming years and Polley would ultimately play a pivotal role in the downfall of this great band, ending in the greatest of tragedies – but we'll get to that later.

As for *No Dice*, it can be viewed realistically as the band's proper full-length debut album, conceived as a complete piece of work rather than a patchwork assemblage of odds and sods. It's no real surprise that this record became the band's best-selling LP, particularly in the US. It's well-crafted and well-produced, offering up a pleasingly balanced collection of old-fashioned rock 'n' rollers, catchy and melodious pop tunes and emotional ballads. With the arrival of Joey Molland, the band starts to form a much clearer musical identity and, instead of twee pop songs rooted in the mid-1960s and baroque pop, we get to hear a much more contemporary sound – melodic, guitar/piano-driven pop-rock. Some fans may mourn the loss of the old 'mixed bag' charm of the previous records, but the overall cohesiveness of this record and the consistent, high-quality songwriting and musicianship on display cannot be denied.

The album was first released on CD in 1992 (with additional bonus tracks) and then again in 2010, as part of Apple's major album reissue campaign, with further bonus tracks spread across both the CD and digital formats.

'I Can't Take It' (Ham)
First worked on at the band's initial recording session with Joey, this harder-edged, rock 'n' roll-style song kicks off the album in fine style. Emitting an energy similar to that generated during their live shows, the band perform admirably on this rocker. Commencing with a guitar riff intro conjured up by Joey, this scintillating number's catchy and urgent beat is relentlessly driven forward by a combination of Mike's impressive skin pounding and some exhilarating guitar work courtesy of both Pete and Joey. Punctuated by occasional bursts of horns that add lustre to the proceedings, the tune also boasts some wonderful, Beatles-style 'Whoo-oo' vocals during the choruses. Pete delivers a confident lead vocal which is nicely complemented by Joey and Tom and their enthusiastic backing vocals.

Although initially worked on with Mal Evans at the production helm, the final album version was produced by Geoff Emerick (in fact, this was actually the very first song that Geoff worked on with the band after taking over production duties) and he does a commendable job recreating the band's live sound. Actual live versions of this song are available on both the band's *BBC In Concert 1972-3* CD (Strange Fruit, 1997) and the *Day After Day – Badfinger Live* album (Rykodisc, 1990). The BBC version (recorded at the Paris Theatre, London, 10 August 1973) is extended in length and played at a faster tempo, resulting in an even more energetic reading of the song, albeit a little ragged in delivery. The *Day After Day* live version (taken from a gig at the Cleveland Agora club, Ohio, 4 March 1974) offers up another great rocking performance of the song [however, it should be noted that the ten-track *Day After Day – Badfinger Live* album (co-produced by Joey Molland) does employ extensive re-recording and overdubbing. For this reason, the release is oft-panned and much-maligned by fans and critics alike, but, personally, I still think it stands as an enjoyable and worthwhile listen even if its audio authenticity has been modified somewhat during post-production].

A previously unreleased extended version of the studio track was also made available on the 2010 Apple Records CD reissue as a bonus track.

'I Don't Mind' (Evans, Molland)

A mid-tempo, more ruminative piece, this rock ballad was officially credited as being a co-write between Joey and Tom. However, Joey disputes this and in Michael A. Cimino's book, *Badfinger and Beyond – The Biography of Joey Molland*, states that:

> Tommy didn't contribute to this song. It was my song. I don't know why Tommy was given credit on this because he did not write any of it.

Well, regardless of writing credits, it's a lovely, lilting little tune with a sweet-sounding melody. For the most part, it's a fairly quiet and sedate number, only briefly bursting into life during the choruses. Joey handles the lead vocals on this one and his voice is treated to produce a nice, echoey effect. Tom and Pete, meanwhile, provide the delightful harmonies which closely follow Joey's lead. Pete also plays piano on this one and delivers a lovely little solo mid-song.

A 'live' version of this song can also be found on the band's *Day After Day – Badfinger Live* album.

'Love Me Do' (Molland)

A back-to-basics, 1950s-style rock 'n' roller, this Joey-penned number is a fun and catchy effort, albeit a little lightweight. The title of the song is Joey's cheeky nod to all those Beatles comparisons that plagued the band at the time. Clearly influenced by the likes of Chuck Berry, it's an enjoyable slice of toe-tapping pop-rock featuring some terrific drum fills from Mike and great lead guitar work from Pete. Joey plays rhythm guitar on this one and also handles lead vocal duties. Whilst his vocal delivery is enthusiastic enough, Joey's voice does stray out of tune slightly at times, although this merely adds to the overall charm of the track.

An instrumental version of the song was made available on Apple Records' 2010 digital reissue of the album as a bonus track.

'Midnight Caller' (Ham)

This tender, heartfelt composition by Pete tells the story of a lonely call girl and was actually inspired by a close friend of the band called Sue Wing, who at one time, before becoming a high-class escort, had been the booking agent for the pre-Badfinger group, The Iveys. An exquisite, piano-based ballad, this tune features a touching, sincere lyric delivered by a sensitive and emotive lead vocal from Pete. Pete's sweet voice is accompanied by Joey and the subtle chiming of his 12-string acoustic guitar, producing a beautifully melancholic vibe. Pete's delicate piano keys and Mike's gentle drums fill out the sound, whilst the band's beautiful harmonious vocals appear towards the end of the song, closing this moving and reflective piece in style.

Pete's solo piano demo version is also available on his *Golders Green* CD.

'No Matter What'* (Ham)

Released as a single A-side (b/w 'Carry On Till Tomorrow' (US), 'Better Days' (UK)): October 1970 (US), chart #8; November 1970 (UK), chart #5

Another of the songs initially worked on at the very first recording session with Joey, the band knew they were onto something special with this one and suggested it to Apple as their new single fairly early on. However, rather puzzlingly, Apple initially rejected it. Thankfully, however, Apple eventually saw the light and realised what a cracking tune it was and gave the track the nod as the lead-off single (with the Mal Evans-produced version getting some additional polish from Geoff Emerick). To help with the promotion of the single, a special promo film was shot at a farm in Wales where the band were busy readying themselves for the forthcoming US tour.

Penned by Pete Ham, this is a classic blast of power-pop perfection. Featuring an irresistibly catchy guitar hook and stupendous vocals, it's an aural delight from start to finish. Whilst Pete came up with the riff idea and provides the basic rhythm, Joey plays the arpeggio over the chords of the song and the riffs behind it. Joey also performs the superb solo on his Firebird guitar. The distinctive (swirling staccato) guitar sounds were created by sending the guitar parts through a slow speed Leslie speaker cabinet and this was apparently Mal Evans' idea (which isn't much of a surprise given Mal's close association with The Beatles, who were famed Leslie speaker experimentalists). The track also boasts another Beatles influence with its fake ending a la 'Hello Goodbye'. Regarding the Beatles inspiration, Joey had this to say in the Michael A. Cimino-authored biography:

It's obvious The Beatles were a big influence on us. They inspired a lot of the things we did. They were the reference point for that kind of music, and those kinds of songs.

Aside from the wonderful guitar sounds, the song is also notable for its amazing vocals. Pete delivers a sensational lead performance whilst Joey and Tom supply the glorious backing harmonies. All in all, it's a tremendously enjoyable slice of guitar-driven power-pop.

A previously unreleased studio demo version of the song was made available on the 2010 CD reissue of the album as a bonus track, whilst a solo acoustic version of the song by Pete Ham was released on his *7 Park Avenue* CD.

'Without You' (Ham, Evans)

Now well established as a classic perennial pop standard, this song originally started out as two individual pieces by Pete Ham and Tom Evans, respectively. Pete had been working on a tune, tentatively entitled 'If It's Love', since 1969. He had the verses pretty much sorted but was struggling to come up with a suitable chorus. Meanwhile, Tom had been working on a song idea called 'I Can't Live' but was suffering from the opposite problem to Pete – he had a great, rousing chorus but was having trouble with his verses. At some point, a decision was made to merge the two incomplete pieces into one and this amalgamation proved to be a complete stroke of genius. What the band ended up creating was hauntingly beautiful and utterly sublime – a dramatic, romantic ballad incorporating Ham's tender and heartfelt verses and Tom's passionate and emotionally charged chorus. The heartbreakingly melancholic melody is also incredibly evocative and memorable.

Interestingly, one of the co-writers was not all that impressed with the composition initially. Tom Evans (from the Dan Matovina-authored band biography) made the following comment:

I couldn't get myself to sing it with real conviction. When we got to the studio, I said, 'I don't like this. It's too corny'. It seemed like such a schmaltzy tune.

The tune was initially worked on in the studio with Mal Evans producing and then again, later on, with Geoff Emerick at the production helm. The song's resultant understated instrumentation is incredibly effective and allows for the naked emotion of the song to shine through. The distinctive guitar solo comes courtesy of Joey and, as stated by Joey in the Cimino-authored biography, was actually worked on by both himself and band manager, Bill Collins. The other standout instrumental segment comes towards the end of the song with the extended keyboard outro that is eerily reminiscent of Procol Harum's 'A Whiter Shade Of Pale'.

Regarding Harry Nilsson's version of the song, Badfinger first became aware of it the following year, in 1971. The band were at a recording studio and Nilsson also happened to be working there. He apparently came and introduced himself to the band and asked them to come and listen to a song he was mixing down the hall, which of course, turned out to be his version of 'Without You'. The Badfinger boys were blown away by what they heard. (Taken from the Matovina book) Pete later recalled:

As soon as we heard it, we knew that was the way we wanted to do it, but never had the nerve.

Tom Evans added:

We were totally paranoid of doing it that way. Nilsson's version really showed what you can do with a song, production-wise, and with a good singer. It blew me away.

Nilsson's version, of course, went on to become a global number one smash the following year and has since become regarded, quite rightly, as an absolute classic. Since then, the song has been covered numerous times by a variety of artists, but the other really notable version came in the 1990s when US pop singer Mariah Carey also achieved a global smash hit with her cover of the song (which was based on the Nilsson arrangement rather than the Badfinger one).

In 1973 (in the wake of Nilsson's success with the song), the song's composers, Pete Ham and Tom Evans, deservedly received two Ivor Novello awards for 'Best Song Musically and Lyrically' and 'International Hit of the Year', respectively, which rightfully recognised and rewarded the musical splendour of this wonderful composition.

Note: The previously unreleased studio demo version of the song (produced by Mal Evans) was issued as a bonus track on the 2010 CD album reissue – whilst this is a rougher, less polished take overall, the strength of the composition is still clearly evident at this early run-through stage. A solo, electric piano demo version of the song 'If It's Love' (Pete's embryonic version of 'Without You', inspired by his girlfriend, Bev Ellis) is also available on Pete's *Golders Green* CD – this is a fascinating listen as it clearly shows that whilst the verses are pretty much in place, Pete is indeed struggling to come up with a suitable chorus. An acoustic guitar demo version of 'If It's Love' can also be found on the bonus CD given away with the first edition of Dan Matovina's band biography. A very interesting, albeit brief, snippet of Tom's 'I Can't Live' demo (which provided the chorus that Pete was looking for to complement his verses of 'If It's Love') was also made available on the bonus CD that accompanied the first edition of the Matovina-authored tome. This little snatch of audio offers a fascinating listen and features a great, lively vocal from Tom, even at this early demo stage.

'Blodwyn' (Ham)

This happy, upbeat, albeit lightweight tune exhibits a somewhat country-folk vibe and lyrically describes an old Welsh custom whereby a boy carves an ornamental spoon out of wood and gives it to a girl that he loves. If the girl accepts the gift, then she effectively accepts the boy – seemingly, this old custom is akin to a proposal of marriage!

Despite the slightly corny nature of the lyric, Pete still delivers a charmingly sincere lead vocal. This extremely pleasant-sounding, mid-tempo ditty also boasts some terrific vocal harmonies during the choruses and the attractive slide guitar parts that punctuate the song add to the overall country-esque charm.

'Better Days' (Evans, Molland)

The second track on the album credited as a co-writing effort between Joey and Tom, this is again disputed by Joey, who has gone on record as stating that Tom didn't have anything to do with the writing of the song. Again, regardless of who actually wrote the tune, it's a very pleasurable, mid-tempo, country-tinged number that features some sterling guitar work from both Joey and Pete whose Chuck Berry-inspired guitar licks really elevate the song. Joey sings lead competently, but the vocal highlight comes towards the end of the track with some delicious 'whoo-oo' harmonies. According to Joey (in the Cimino-authored biography), he wrote the song with Elvis Presley in mind and pictured the King performing it, adding that the band also wanted to get a feel for the song similar to that of The Band's 'Up On Cripple Creek'. However, Joey also confirmed in the same source that Mike Gibbins struggled to get this 'feel' and that the underlying tension between Mike and Tom reared its head during the recording of this track:

> ...Tommy was goading him a bit. Mike got angry and left. This is three sessions into recording with the band! To my knowledge, Tommy and Mike were at loggerheads all the time. Tommy was not all that enamoured of Mike's drumming.

A live version of this track can be found on the band's *BBC In Concert* album (recorded at the Paris Theatre, London, 8 June 1972). This version is played at a faster tempo and performed in a looser fashion than its studio counterpart, but it's a great energetic performance and the song ultimately ends up sounding punchier in this live setting.

'It Had To Be' (Gibbins)

Although written by Mike, Pete Ham helped out his bandmate on this one by sorting the arrangement and singing the lead vocal. His strong, emotive voice impresses and is complemented nicely by the other boys' backing harmonies. It's a slower tempo, ballad-style composition that reveals Mike's more contemplative side. Short and sweet, this gentle, swaying, melodious tune also boasts some nice, blended guitar parts, courtesy of Joey and Pete.

'Watford John' (Evans, Molland, Ham, Gibbins)
Starting off as a group studio jam, this track was eventually developed into a fully formed composition. An ode to John Smith, an Apple Studios engineer from, err, Watford, this track betrays its beginnings with its rather spontaneous, loose feel. The tune kicks off with some tasty boogie-style piano before Pete's confident lead vocal takes flight. The throwback, rock 'n' roll beat is then enlivened by some sizzling guitar licks that pervade the track. The song loses its way slightly towards the end as it meanders in search of a definitive conclusion but it's still, ultimately, a joyous musical romp.

'Believe Me'* (Evans)
Another track initially worked on at the first recording session with Joey, this tune unashamedly exudes a late-Beatles vibe (in particular, there are strong shades of 'Oh! Darling' on this one). Tom sings the lead vocal splendidly, with convincing passion, and there are nice, complimentary backing harmonies from Pete and Joey. Interestingly, Tom plays the main guitar lick on this one whilst Joey provides the bass work.

The dual guitar solos come courtesy of Joey and Pete and supplement the track nicely. The additional instrumental accompaniment comes in the shape of some understated piano work (courtesy of Pete), subtle and supportive drum beats (from Mike) and a sprinkling of prominent, characterful percussion throughout.

A previously unreleased alternative version of the song was made available on the 2010 CD reissue as a bonus track.

'We're For The Dark' (Ham)
The album comes to a close with this impressive Pete Ham composition. The title of the track was apparently lifted by Pete from Shakespeare's *Anthony and Cleopatra* play. Acoustic-based, this song is constructed around a fairly subtle and simple arrangement which allows the natural beauty of the tune to shine through. Boasting a sweet and engaging melody, this tune successfully evokes a great sense of romanticism.

The song begins delicately with the chiming sound of a strummed Spanish guitar before Pete's warm and earnest voice starts up, instantly beguiling the listener. The graceful, folk-pop foundation is then built upon mid-song with the introduction of some lush orchestration, initially with strings and then finally with the horn section, all culminating in an epic fusion of vocals and instrumentation before calm is restored and the track elegantly fades out. The production and arrangement work on this track is to be commended as a perfect balance is achieved with the orchestration adding a richness and fullness to the acoustic base without ever overpowering it.

A live version of this song is available on the band's *BBC In Concert 1972-3* album (recorded at the Paris Theatre, London, 8 June 1972).

Other Contemporary Songs
'Get Down' (Evans, Gibbins, Ham, Molland)
One of the songs initially worked on at the first session with Joey, this was eventually left off the final album and shelved. This is a shame because it's actually a great little guitar-driven rocker. Similar to 'Watford John', this is a group jam-style effort and boasts some absolutely sizzling guitar work throughout and some really terrific vocal work (Joey and Tom both impress on shared lead vocals).

The Geoff Emerick-produced version was actually issued as a bonus track on the 1992 CD reissue of the album, whilst the earlier Mal Evans-produced version was eventually released as a bonus track on the 2010 digital reissue of the album (Mal's version actually rocks harder and heavier than the Emerick take. It's also longer and really shows off the song's insistent groove).

'Friends Are Hard To Find' (aka 'Photograph')* (Molland)
Again, one of the songs first worked on with Joey, this track was originally entitled 'Photograph' but was later renamed. As with 'Get Down', this too didn't make the original album tracklisting and was initially shelved. According to Joey (from the Cimino biography), the song was about an old friend of his:

> I was thinking about a girl named Michelle I had met when I was with Gary Walker & the Rain. She was a friend of Gary's and we had gone out a couple of times. I was thinking about her and how nice it would be to find her. I had her photograph, but I couldn't get in touch with her, and I wrote a song about it.

Again, it's a shame that this track didn't make the final tracklisting, as it's a really enjoyable slice of pop rock. There is some sterling electric guitar work throughout and some solid skin-pounding from Mike. The extended, hypnotic fade-out is also particularly effective, with the vocal harmonies, guitars and drums all blending beautifully into the fade-out. Joey even cheekily borrows from The Beatles' 'A Day In The Life' for the opening line of some of his verses – 'Well, I had to laugh, I saw the photograph' – sadly, according to Joey, Apple were just not all that impressed with the track!

Thankfully, however, this track did eventually see the light of day, first seeing a release as a bonus track on the 1992 CD reissue of the album and then again as a bonus track on the 2010 CD reissue, this time in the form of an alternate extended stereo mix.

'Live, Love All Of Your Days' (Ham)

Displaying a gospel and soul influence, this high-quality, mid-tempo Pete Ham-penned demo number boasts a very likeable and upbeat melody. Short and sweet, this home demo is available on Pete's 7 *Park Avenue* CD.

'Dear Father' (Ham)

Another Pete Ham home demo from the period, this is a quieter and more thoughtful piece. Pete's voice is sweet, tender and sincere as he croons over yet another strongly defined melody, albeit one that is more rooted in the mid-1960s. This home demo is also available on the 7 *Park Avenue* CD.

'Leaving On A Midnight Train' (Ham)

Another Pete Ham-composed demo track, this one's a good-time rocker that exhibits a nice blues/boogie feel. This is one track that you can really envisage the rest of the band on. A Badfinger version would surely have produced one rollicking and stomping effort. As it is, the Pete Ham home demo is available on the 7 *Park Avenue* CD.

'Hand In Hand' (Ham)

Yet another Ham-penned demo from the period, this one features a slightly dated sound coupled with somewhat corny lyrics about the usual lovey-dovey stuff. Having said that, it's still likeable, catchy fluff and would probably have been a big hit in the mid-1960s! This home demo is again available on the 7 *Park Avenue* album.

'Sille Veb' (Ham)

Recorded by Pete as a Christmas present for his girlfriend of the time, Bev Ellis – the title is her name spelt backwards – this sweet-sounding tune boasts an exquisite melody and a fine, poignant and emotional vocal delivery from the composer. Once again, this home demo is available on the 7 *Park Avenue* album.

'Pete's Walk' (Ham)

This short and sweet instrumental from Pete features some wonderfully distorted and fuzzy-sounding electric guitar. A meandering, riff-filled snippet of a tune, this shows off Pete's terrific guitar skills. The home demo of this track is available on Pete's *Golders Green* CD album.

'Goodbye John Frost' (Ham)

This is yet another home demo from the period penned by the incredibly prolific Pete Ham. This jaunty little piano-based number, reminiscent of The Beatles' 'Ob-La-Di, Ob-La-Da' at times, is a real buoyant and perky ditty that readily puts a smile on the face of the listener. A toe-tapping romp of a tune – thoroughly enjoyable. This demo can also be found on Pete's *Golders Green* album.

'Where Will You Be' (Ham)

A beautiful, haunting composition from the pen of Pete Ham, this superbly atmospheric track features a truly wonderful lead vocal from Pete combined with exquisite, late-Beatles-style harmonies. Lyrically and melodically, this is incredibly strong stuff and the end result is goosebump-inducing. This home demo is also available on the *Golders Green* album.

Straight Up

Personnel:
Pete Ham: vocals, guitars, keyboards, percussion
Tom Evans: vocals, bass
Joey Molland: vocals, guitars
Mike Gibbins: vocals, drums, percussion
Additional musicians
George Harrison: guitar ('Day After Day', 'I'd Die Babe')
Leon Russell: piano ('Day After Day'), 'car horn' guitar ('Suitcase')
Klaus Voormann: electric piano ('Suitcase')
Bill Collins: accordion ('Sweet Tuesday Morning')
Nicky Bell: percussion ('Perfection')
Recorded at Abbey Road, Trident, Morgan, Command and AIR Studios, London, UK
(January-October 1971)
Produced by Todd Rundgren and *George Harrison (and **Geoff Emerick)
UK release date: February 1972
US release date: December 1971
Highest chart places: UK: Did not chart, US: 31

From January through to February of 1971, the band, together with producer
Geoff Emerick, hastily worked on the follow-up album to *No Dice* in a
number of different London-based recording studios. With an impending US
tour due to start in early March, the resultant album presented to Apple was,
unsurprisingly, a little rushed and rough around the edges. Whilst on tour in
America (which went reasonably well, with the band performing a mixture
of old and new material interspersed with old, rock 'n' roll covers), their
Apple paymasters deliberated over the new album and the proposed new
single, a track called 'Name Of The Game'. Disappointingly, upon their return
to the UK in mid-May, the band discovered that both the album and single
had been rejected. Joey Molland's recollection in the Matovina-authored
tome is that Apple rejected the album because it was 'too much like a beat
group,' although in the liner notes to the 1993 CD reissue of the album, he
elaborated further:

> The tapes sounded like they were recorded properly, but I think Apple thought
> they were a bit crude. They wanted us to go in for an *Abbey Road*-type sound.

This sentiment echoes other sources that suggest certain people at Apple were
not happy with Geoff Emerick's production work on the record. As a result,
Apple wanted a new producer to work with the band and ultimately ended
up asking George Harrison if he'd be interested in the job, a proposal the ex-
Beatle readily accepted. However, just before work with George commenced,
some of the Badfinger boys were busy helping out another ex-Beatle – Joey
Molland and Tom Evans had been recruited by John Lennon to help out on a

few tracks for his new *Imagine* album and ended up playing acoustic guitars on both 'Jealous Guy' and 'I Don't Want To Be A Soldier'.

Recording sessions with George Harrison took place at Abbey Road Studios and began towards the end of May. A couple of the songs from the rejected album were re-done and a couple of new songs were also initiated. However, these sessions only lasted for a few weeks before George soon became involved in the organisation of the now-legendary *Concert for Bangladesh* (a pair of benefit concerts put together to raise both awareness and funds for the crises prevalent in Bangladesh at that time). Unfortunately, for the band, this meant that George would not be able to continue assisting the band in the studio but, as a form of recompense, he did invite the band to perform at the benefit concerts as part of the house band (with Pete also getting to share the spotlight with George when they duetted on a rendition of 'Here Comes The Sun').

Recording sessions for the album started up again in late September, this time with Todd Rundgren at the production helm. Rundgren, ex-Nazz member and burgeoning solo star in his own right, had also just recently engineered The Band's *Stage Fright* LP. Todd subsequently established an entirely different approach in the studio – working in a very fast and intense manner – and proved a quite different proposition to the band in the studio compared with the likes of Mal Evans and Geoff Emerick. Allegedly, there was some friction in the studio between Todd and the band due to his working methods, but he was there to do a job and that was to ensure the prompt, satisfactory completion of the album. In a whirlwind two-week period, older songs from the earlier recording sessions were either rejigged or completely restarted and some completely new material was also recorded. By November, the album had been mixed and was ready to go. In an interview with *The Hollywood Reporter* in 2013, Todd Rundgren reflected on the recording of the *Straight Up* record:

'Oh geez, let's just get this thing wrapped up somehow!' was essentially the mandate. It seemed to me that they had spent enough time working on the record and that they really needed to get it done. It wasn't so much focusing on any one or another track to make sure that they would make good singles. The band had something of a sensibility for that anyway … I got two batches of tapes: the ones that George had worked on and the ones that Geoff Emerick had worked on, and they sounded like two completely different records. The intention had been that George was going to do a complete record with them using that au courant sound that was going around at the time, [a la] Phil Spector, that involved five or six acoustic guitars playing all the time, double-tracked drums and all kinds of stuff to make it sound really big. But everything that you produce with that style tends to sound the same. I was a little more interested in actually moving a little closer to what Geoff Emerick was doing, which was trying to capture what the band actually sounded like. A lot of the George Harrison mixes, I stripped stuff out or replaced things, because it sounded like a George Harrison record, just with other people singing the vocals. In the end, you didn't want the record to leave people with the impression that the record was from three different sets of sessions.

Joey Molland also later reflected on the band's experience of working with Rundgren in an October 2020 interview with *Guitar World*:

He didn't really think about what he was going to say before he said it – he just said it. He was very rude, actually, and we didn't like him. We were quite happy when it was over. He went away and took the tapes; we never did overdubs or anything. He took the tracks that George had done and mixed them. We just heard the record when it came out.

The responsibility for the new LP's sleeve design again fell to Richard DiLello and Gene Mahon (who had also worked on the previous *No Dice* record sleeve). This time around, they came up with a very simple and straightforward portrait shot of the band for the front cover, with the rather joyless-looking members decked out in brown leather and suede jackets – hardly the most striking of album covers! As for the title of the new album, reports vary as to whether it was Tom Evans or Richard DiLello who came up with *Straight Up*.

With the album in the bag, the band filled out the remaining October-December period with several UK gigs. 'Day After Day' was then released as the first single from the new album in November (in the US), with the parent album being released the following month. Corresponding releases in the UK occurred in January and February, respectively, of the following year. Contemporary reviews were surprisingly mixed and, if anything, leaned slightly more to the negative side. The following reviews offer some insight into the general critical reception at the time – *Rolling Stone*:

Straight Up is a big disappointment coming after Badfinger's previous superb album, *No Dice* ... the result here is self-consciousness in place of spontaneity, solemnity in the place of formal exuberance and a general all-around deadness where infectious energy was previously the rule.

Mike Saunders, the author of this particular review, filled out the remaining page space with similar scathing criticism bemoaning the record's lack of rock 'n' roll energy and spirit, lack of melodies and inferior production – somebody clearly got out of bed the wrong side that day! *Disc and Music Echo*, meanwhile, continued with the ever-present Beatles comparisons:

Badfinger's sound is that of the Beatles in the *Rubber Soul* era without the Beatles' magic exuberance ... The Beatles similarities strike you all the time ... 'Day After Day' is so like 'I Feel Fine' you almost fall off your seat...

The review continues in this vein complaining that the album 'doesn't have enough light and shade' before concluding that:

> They write neat songs, are musically competent … At the moment, though, they're a little too tight reined and unspontaneous.

Creem magazine was similarly unenthusiastic in its critique of the new record:

> On *Straight Up*, Badfinger have chosen to consolidate and show off their sound, a curiously bland and unremarkable blend of guitars, drums, and nubile voices that really doesn't go anywhere or in much of a blaze of hurry … Badfinger would be better off doing twelve of the Beatles' greatest hits and doing them without all this pretension of originality.

Thankfully, expressing more positivity in its outlook, *Stereo Review* had this to say:

> With this album, Badfinger grows … *Straight Up* isn't a classic like the Bee Gees *Horizontal* or the Hollies *Evolution*, but it is an enjoyable celebration of one of the healthiest kinds of rock.

Reassuringly, retrospective assessments have been far kinder and the album is now regarded as something of a 'classic,' and there are many fans who consider it as the band's finest work. Stephen Thomas Erlewine's *Allmusic* review sums up the more modern critical thinking:

> Here, there's absolutely no filler and everybody is in top form. Pete Ham's 'Baby Blue' is textbook power pop… what holds the record together is Joey Molland's emergence as a songwriter … fine songwriting, combined with sharp performances and exquisite studio craft, make *Straight Up* one of the cornerstones of power pop.

Thankfully, the record-buying public ignored the critics and a sense of good taste prevailed globally. By early 1972, the band had both a hit single and album on their hands. The single was a Top Ten smash hit on both sides of the Atlantic, whilst the album just missed out on a Top Thirty placing in the US *Billboard* charts. Again, album sales stalled somewhat in the band's domestic market, but I would imagine that the same issues as before were the reason for this – disarray/disinterest within Apple UK and the British perception of the band as being more of a 'singles' band than an 'album' band.

Whilst on their third US tour, a second single was lifted from the new album and released in the States. 'Baby Blue' proved another popular hit with the band's US fans, peaking at #14 in the *Billboard* charts (again, it's interesting to note that this song was also originally scheduled for a UK release but, for some reason, was cancelled). The US tour (February-April 1972) was a success, with many dates selling out. This was closely followed by a UK tour in May/June before yet another tour of the US from June-August. By this time, Nilsson's version of 'Without You' had also become a global smash and the band's career was at its zenith.

As for my take on *Straight Up*, I do think it's a great album overall. However, in my humble opinion, it's not their best complete piece of work – that would come a few years later on another record label – but it's still a high-quality musical affair filled to the brim with prime cuts of impeccably crafted power-pop tunes and stately ballads. There's very little in the way of filler material and Todd Rundgren's overall production is unarguably slick. The final tracklisting is also superior to that of the rejected (Geoff Emerick-produced) offering. There may not be quite as much stylistic variety on the final record (with the rejected album being closer in dynamic spirit to the previous *No Dice* album), but the final LP presents a more balanced listening experience with more musical and lyrical maturity (interestingly, Geoff Emerick did receive a 'Special Thanks' credit on the final, released album). Apparently, it was Todd Rundgren's decision to go with a majority of slower to mid-tempo numbers and certain critics (such as *Rolling Stone*'s Mike Saunders!) did accuse the record of lacking a certain vitality, but I think Todd (and George Harrison to a lesser extent) and the band ended up creating a very fine record of understated splendour.

The album was released on CD for the first time in 1993 (with bonus tracks) and then reissued again in 2010 (as part of Apple's major reissue campaign) in CD and digital formats with additional bonus tracks spread across both formats.

'Take It All' (Ham)

The album opener, a stately, keyboard-driven, mid-tempo number, was written by Pete Ham in the wake of the *Concert for Bangladesh* and serves as a very personal response to being thrust into the limelight (when he was 'selected' over others in the band to duet with George Harrison). A melancholic piano intro sets the appropriate mood for the piece before Pete's vocals kick in, whereupon he delivers the meditative lyrics in convincingly impassioned style. Indeed, at times, Pete really sounds like he's straining to reach some of the notes, but this just adds to the raw emotional power of his voice throughout this song. Tom Evans also contributes to the powerful vocal sound by delivering some sublime, higher-pitched backing vocals, which reinforce the emotional impact of the song. Mike provides a solid backbeat over which Pete's keyboard skills are allowed to shine. The piano fills are great, but it's the organ solo mid-song that provides a real aural treat.

A live version of this song is available on the band's *BBC In Concert 1972-3* album (recorded at the Paris Theatre, London, 8 June 1972), which presents a fairly faithful reproduction of the studio version, albeit with a guitar solo replacing the keyboard solo. Also, a rough Pete Ham (keyboard) demo version was made available on the bonus CD that accompanied the second edition of the Matovina-authored Badfinger biography. Even though it's just a demo run-through, Pete's vocal delivery is impressively top-notch throughout (although at this early stage, the chorus and final verse are incomplete).

'Baby Blue' (Ham)
Released as a single A-side (b/w 'Flying'): March 1972 (US), chart #14

One of the first 'new' songs worked on with Todd Rundgren now in the producer's seat, this majestic composition from the pen of Pete Ham was written for his new girlfriend at the time, Dixie (who even gets namechecked in the song a couple of times). Pete had met Dixie during the early US tour of 1971 and the pair had enjoyed a whirlwind romance, but it had been short-lived due to Pete returning to the UK after the completion of the tour. He had, however, promised to stay in touch with her, but, as Pete later confessed, he hadn't exactly been true to his word and subsequently feared that she would be angry with him for not writing or calling after he'd left the US and returned home. He, therefore, ended up writing 'Baby Blue' about this situation:

> All that time without a word
> Didn't know you'd think that I'd forget or I'd regret
> The special love I had for you, my baby blue

This stirring and irresistibly catchy, fuzz riff-filled beauty of a song delivers on pretty much every level. The musicianship throughout is utterly superb – Pete's choppy and forceful rhythm guitar, Joey's crisp and elegant lead guitar, Mike's simple yet solid, early-1960s drumbeat, all glued together by Tom's bass foundation. The vocals are also spot on – Pete's beautifully heartfelt and earnest lead closely tracked by an equally emotive Tom on backing vox. This track really is a prime example of the band's unique musical chemistry and shows everyone what they were truly capable of. Even the song's composer himself was quite rightly proud of this one. From a June 1972 Canadian radio interview (on CHUM radio), Pete had this to say:

> It was just a very personal thing. To me, it was one of the few songs that I thought was whole and complete. I mean, you write a song and people think, 'oh, that's nice' or whatever, but you never quite think, well, I made it on that song 100%, you know, but Baby Blue, to me, I almost made it.

Although released as a single in many territories around the world (including the US where it became another sizeable hit for the band), its planned release in the UK mysteriously never came to be, which is a real shame as I'm sure it would have provided the band with another domestic smash hit. As for the US single mix (by Al Steckler, head of Apple's US operations), the most discernible difference is the more defined drum sound (courtesy of a reverberated snare drum). This single mix was released as a bonus track on both the 1993 and 2010 CD reissues of the album. Meanwhile, a 'live' version of this melancholic, power-pop ballad is also available on the *Day After Day – Badfinger Live* album (which presents a fairly faithful reproduction of the studio version).

This song actually experienced a well-deserved resurgence of popularity in 2013 when it was featured prominently during the closing scene of the final ever episode of the popular TV show, *Breaking Bad*. A lot of people in the US and UK subsequently downloaded/streamed the track after that final episode and, as a result, the song even made it into the UK singles chart for the first time ever, peaking at #73. In the wake of this resurgence, producer Todd Rundgren made the following comments (in a 2013 interview with *The Hollywood Reporter*) regarding the recording of the song:

> 'Baby Blue' was the first new track that we actually recorded. I was putting a guitar through a Leslie [amplifier], which was designed for an organ, so it got this kind of swirly guitar sound that was somewhat signature on the song. But in terms of, did we think this was a hit or that's a hit or whatever? I recall it more being a question of, 'Let's just finish it somehow!'

'Money' (Evans)

Originally recorded with Geoff Emerick and then, later, re-recorded with Todd Rundgren, this moody Tom Evans composition finds him ruminating on money as the proverbial root of all evil! The final LP version features a nice, chiming (Byrds-esque) guitar sound throughout and shows off a fine vocal fusion of Tom and Joey's voices. The original version features less Byrds-like guitar and also includes some rich and luxurious, George Martin-arranged orchestration.

During the Emerick sessions, it was decided to medley 'Money' with another track, 'Flying'. On the original, rejected LP, the two songs were bridged by stirring George Martin-arranged orchestral parts. However, on the subsequent Todd Rundgren version, this segue into the 'Flying' track is far more subtle with its stripped-back approach.

The Geoff Emerick version was released as a bonus track on both the 1993 CD reissue and 2010 digital reissue of the album.

'Flying' (Molland, Evans)

The second part of the album's medley, this tune was written whilst on the band's first US tour with lyrical inspiration coming from certain band members and their consumption of LSD! Tom and Joey again share vocal duties on this one and their harmonisation is wonderful. For the final, released LP version, Todd Rundgren essentially re-mixed the Emerick-produced version and sped it up in order to match the key of the previous track, 'Money'.

The noticeable differences between the two versions, at least to my ears, are that the drums are more prominent (the piano less so) and Joey's vocals more clearly defined in the original version. Also, in this original version, the vocals are slightly phased at the beginning, Lennon-style, whilst the fade-out on the Rundgren-produced version has a richer, fuller fusion of piano, guitar, percussion and voice. The track, undeniably, exudes a Beatles-y vibe, not just in sound but also with regards to the opposing lyrical content of the song's two composers. Here, Joey's first verse is happier and more positive in outlook (see McCartney), whereas Tom's second verse delivers a more acerbic and cynical lyric (see Lennon), but it makes for an appealing contrast.

The Geoff Emerick-produced version was released as a bonus track on both the 1993 CD reissue and 2010 digital reissue of the album.

'I'd Die, Babe'* (Molland)
This Joey Molland-penned slice of guitar-driven pop-rock was not only produced and arranged by George Harrison, but it also features some distinctive guitar work from the ex-Beatle in the form of the song's riffs (George also helps out Joey on acoustic guitar). Pete Ham supplies the piano work and sterling overdubbed lead guitar. Displaying a faster tempo than most of the other songs on the record, it's a real catchy, toe-tapping number. Joey's lead vocal delivery is confident and there's some nice, complimentary backing from Tom. All in all, it's a fun and thoroughly enjoyable track.

As for working with George Harrison, Joey looked back fondly on the experience in an interview with *Guitar World* (October 2020):

He was great as a producer. He was great at everything he did with us. He was very communicative. If he had an idea to change an arrangement, he would sit down and talk to you about it. He always had a good reason for doing something, but he wanted you to feel good about it. He was a very good producer in every way.

It should, however, also be noted that Todd Rundgren was responsible for the actual final mix that appeared on the LP.

'Name of the Game'* (Ham)
A cornerstone of the album, this masterful Ham-penned composition finds its author in a particularly pensive and reflective mood. The almost impenetrable, complex lyrics reveal a young man with an emotional maturity beyond his years and probably concern a number of personal issues Pete was dealing with at the time.

The original, Geoff Emerick-produced version of this majestic pop ballad starts off with a gentle, yet insistent acoustic strum, which is soon joined by Pete's earnest vocal. The sound builds with the subtle introduction of strings in the background, gradually peaking in the chorus with the dramatic appearance of the horn section. The second half of the song sees the continued presence of the stirring orchestral parts reinforcing the acoustic foundation and enhancing the dramatic power of the track. A sense of calm is restored at the end as the acoustic-orchestral fusion slowly fades out. It's terrific stuff and not at all surprising that this tune was strongly considered as a possible single at the time. However, despite several attempts at remixing the song by various people (including the combined talents of George Harrison and Phil Spector at one point), the song was ultimately rejected as a single.

A little later, when George Harrison was officially on board as producer, he again decided to work on the song with the band and actually re-recorded the track. With a new arrangement emphasising the exquisite and intricate melody, the Harrison version was also slowed down and extended. This version also saw the benefit of George's experience with vocal harmonies as the band's superlative harmonising is simply stunning. This final LP version (ostensibly Harrison's production work, although Todd Rundgren was responsible for the actual final mix and it is possible that he also added some additional overdubs when working with the band) also features prominent piano work throughout which, together with the other delicately played instrumentation, adds an air of classy sophistication to the piece. Pete's lead vocal exudes warmth and strength throughout and lends the contemplative lyric a believable sincerity.

Overall, this LP version offers a more subtle and elegant presentation of the song with everything perfectly balanced, from the understated verses to the dramatic-sounding choruses. It's all very slick and rather impressive, a band clearly at the top of their game. However, I do have a soft spot for the original, Geoff Emerick-produced version, though, as I am a complete sucker for orchestral overdubs in pop-rock songs (I mean, I'm even a fan of The Doors' *Soft Parade* album!). But, if I'm being totally honest, I would admit that maybe, just maybe, the added orchestration in the original version is probably a tad overpowering overall, and Mr Harrison (and Mr Rundgren) probably got it right later on!

The Geoff Emerick version of the track was released as a bonus track on both the 1993 CD reissue and 2010 CD reissue of the album. A 'live' version of this song is also available on the *Day After Day – Badfinger Live* album and offers a very pleasant, guitar-led version of the tune.

'Suitcase'* (Molland)

Another song recorded twice, once with Geoff Emerick and then again with George Harrison, and another which subsequently offers two quite distinctly different versions. Inspired during the band's 1970 UK tour, this is Joey's meditation on the band's life on the road. The original Emerick version presents the track with an appealingly 'dirtier' and heavier rock feel, all wrapped up in a deliciously gritty guitar sound. Less smooth and polished than the subsequent re-recording with George Harrison, this is a really enjoyable slice of foot-stomping, guitar-driven pop-rock. The lead guitar on the original version comes courtesy of Joey.

As for the later re-recording with Harrison at the production helm, we end up with a far more sanitised version of the track, musically and lyrically. In this, the final LP version, we not only get a change of musicians (Pete Ham plays slide guitar, special guest Leon Russell provides 'car horn' guitar whilst Klaus Voormann provides some electric piano – Joey later stated in the Cimino-authored biography that all he did on this version was 'hit the pickup'!), but also an amended lyric. Apparently, George Harrison insisted on 'pusher, pusher' being changed, subsequently becoming 'butcher, butcher', in order to avoid any 'drug' connotations! What this second version does truly benefit from, though, is the incredibly distinctive 'car horn' guitar provided by Leon Russell, whereby his characterful stabs of guitar infuse the track with an engaging bluesy feel. Interestingly, in the liner notes accompanying the 1993 CD reissue of the album, Joey had this to say regarding George Harrison's (and Todd Rundgren's) production work:

The feel of the album changed totally. George started all that. Take one track, 'Suitcase', for instance, if you listen to the first version, the difference between the two is night and day – but the original is much more like Badfinger!

Either way, both versions have their attractive qualities, not least of which are Joey's vocals. He delivers a strong and confident lead vocal on both versions, although the backing vocals are more evident on the Harrison-produced version. Again, it should just be noted that Todd Rundgren was responsible for the actual final mix that appeared on the released record.

The Geoff Emerick version was released as a bonus track on both the 1993 CD reissue and the 2010 digital reissue of the album. There are also two live versions of this track available on the band's *BBC In Concert 1972-3* album (recorded at the Paris Theatre, London, on 8 June 1972 and 10 August 1973, respectively) – both versions are terrific, but the 1972 concert performance, in particular, blows the proverbial roof off. It's an absolutely stonking, near-eight-minute version which shows off the band's superb live musicianship, especially the guitar work of Joey and Pete – exhilarating stuff!

'Sweet Tuesday Morning' (Molland)
Another Molland composition, this sweet-sounding, acoustic-based tune was written about Joey's future wife, Kathie Wiggins, whom he'd met on the band's first US tour. Originally cut with Geoff Emerick at the production helm, the final LP version appeared in a remixed form with additional overdubs. The overdubs were generally of a percussive nature but a notable accordion solo, courtesy of band manager Bill Collins, was also added at the end of the song. This love song is perfectly charming and Joey delivers a sweet and sensitive lead vocal, backed by some beautifully plucked acoustic guitars that are redolent of chiming mandolins at times. The ringing percussive overdubs also add plenty of character to the piece.

The original Geoff Emerick version of the song was released as a bonus track on the 2010 digital reissue of the album. A live version is also available on the band's *BBC In Concert 1972-3* album (and sounds very much like the original Emerick-produced studio recording).

'Day After Day'* (Ham)
Released as a single A-side (b/w 'Money' (US), 'Sweet Tuesday Morning' (UK)): November 1971 (US), chart #4; January 1972 (UK), chart #10
The lead-off single from the album, this is one of the band's most well-known and popular songs. Featuring a memorable slide guitar duet courtesy of George Harrison and Pete Ham, this melodic slice of pop balladry also boasts a strong, confident and note-perfect lead vocal performance from Pete, ably supported by some blissfully divine backing harmonies from the rest of the band. Leon Russell once again guests, this time laying down some wonderful, tinkling piano fills. Tom and Mike provide the steady backbeat whilst Joey supplies the acoustic rhythm.

An air of romantic melancholia pervades the track, with Pete's lyrics probably being informed by his recent relationship woes with his girlfriend, Bev Ellis. The beautifully compelling melody lingers in the listener's mind long after the music has ceased playing and that probably helps explain the enduring popularity of this particular band number. It's also no surprise that the single went on to become such a big hit, ultimately achieving gold sales status with the RIAA (Recording Industry Association of America).

Again, as with the other Harrison-produced tracks, the actual final mix of the track was overseen by Todd Rundgren (and again, it is possible that he also recorded additional overdubs for the track when he was working with the band).

A 'live' version of the song is available on the *Day After Day – Badfinger Live* album, which presents a solid enough performance but one which, unsurprisingly, lacks the finesse of the studio cut. Joey Molland later commented on the difficulties of performing the song live (in a 2014 interview with *Something Else!*):

> It made us a little paranoid, actually. We couldn't do 'Day After Day' anything like the record. We ended up not doing it on stage or only once in a while. It got to be impossible to play, so we'd do other ones. The crowds never said anything to us. I'm sure some people would miss it, but that we just couldn't do it. We didn't want to do a shitty version. They hear the record and that's what they expect.

'Sometimes' (Molland)
This Molland-penned, guitar-based rocker makes for a nice change of pace after the majority of mid-tempo and ballad-type numbers so far. Undeniably, it again echoes that Beatles' mid-1960s sound with its guitar sounds (albeit, they are great) and Mike's simple, yet remarkably solid, drumming performance. Joey's lead vocals are terrific and the background vocal harmonies are also a delight. It's a great little rock 'n' roll tune, performed enthusiastically by all concerned.

'Perfection' (Ham)

This Pete Ham composition slows things back down again after the preceding track. This was another of the songs attempted twice, with different producers. Both versions offer an acoustic foundation, but whereas the original, Geoff Emerick-produced effort notably utilises a Moog synthesiser to enhance the instrumental backing, the Todd Rundgren production opts for a huge dollop of percussion (most of which was played by the band's roadie, Nicky Bell, on this one) and nice, choral-style backing harmonies. The original version, whilst more simple and less fussy overall, also offers a nice harmonica fade-out courtesy of Pete. The Rundgren version, instead, ends with a superlative guitar riff. Joey plays a great electric guitar solo in both versions and Pete's lead vocals are equally terrific on both recordings. The strummed, acoustic intro to both versions is also pretty similar and, to my ears, sounds like a slowed-down version of the intro to 'No Matter What'!

Lyrically, the song was written by Pete as a response to experiencing the ghettos whilst out on tour in the US and generally concern the recognition of one's imperfections and attempting to do something about them.

The Geoff Emerick version of the song was released as a bonus track on both the 1993 CD reissue and 2010 digital reissue of the album.

'It's Over' (Evans)

By this stage, Tom was already struggling to maintain his previously prolific level of songwriting and this would remain the pattern for the next few albums, with Pete and Joey primarily picking up the slack. However, that said, this Evans composition is an absolute belter. Written as a response to the completion of an exhausting US tour, this tune stands as a fine album closer.

Beginning with an attractive fusion of drum and guitar and soon accompanied by rolling piano and choirboy vocal harmonies, the song then gives way to Tom's world-weary vocal delivery as he begins to sing a fond farewell to his American fans. Mike's reliably solid drumming drives the song along, over which ride flourishes of tinkling piano and concise guitar. Come the chorus, and Tom lets rip with his impassioned vocals. Pete Ham plays lead guitar throughout and performs a reliably terrific solo mid-song. Again, the shadow of The Beatles looms large over this song, but, of course, that's no bad thing!

Other Contemporary Songs
'I'll Be The One'** (Ham, Evans, Molland, Gibbins)

This group composition was initially considered as a follow-up single to 'No Matter What' and even went as far as having a radio mix prepared. Sadly, however, for whatever reason, this never happened, which is a real shame because this has 'hit radio song' written all over it. It's an infectiously catchy and perky, country-tinged pop-rocker that ticks all the right boxes – great vocal harmonies, impressive musicianship, a toe-tappingly memorable melody – the ingredients are all there for a hit single! Although originally included on the rejected Geoff Emerick-produced album, I'm not sure it would have suited the final *Straight Up* record, but as a standalone single, it would have been great!

This tune was released as a bonus track on both the 1992 CD reissue of *No Dice* and the 2010 CD reissue of *Straight Up*.

'No Good At All'** (Evans)

This terrific little rocker from the pen of Tom Evans is an absolute blast. Kicking off with a heavy, fuzzed-up guitar intro redolent of the intro to T. Rex's 1971 stomper, 'Get It On', Tom Evans proceeds to deliver a full-throated vocal performance that isn't all that far removed from Slade's Noddy Holder. With the song's insistent and catchy refrain of 'Na, na, na, na, na,' it serves as a little nod of the head to the burgeoning glam-rock scene in the UK at that time. Energetic drumming and great lead guitar work help maintain the song's forward momentum for its brief, just over two-minute runtime. This was another song originally included on the rejected Geoff Emerick-produced album (and eventually saw the light of day when it was released as a bonus track on the 2010 CD reissue of the album).

'Baby Please'** (Ham, Molland, Gibbins)

Whilst Tom was absent from this particular recording session (probably due to illness), Pete, Joey and Mike started jamming and ultimately came up with this offering. Lively, buoyant fun, this energetic little pop-rocker features Joey on bass and rhythm guitars, Pete on lead guitar and Mike on usual drum duty. Pete's guitar work provides a sizzling highlight of the tune and his enthusiastic vocals are a real treat too. This is the sound of a band having a lot of fun in the studio. If I'm to be overly critical, I would say that, ultimately, the track sounds a little loose and throwaway (which is no real surprise, given its 'jam' genesis) and it was probably the right decision to abandon this track and leave it off the *Straight Up* record (despite its original inclusion on the rejected Geoff Emerick-produced album offering) as it sounds more like a B-side to me. The track was ultimately released as a bonus track on the 2010 CD reissue of the album.

'Mean Mean Jemima'** (Molland)

This Joey-penned number is really rather enjoyable. Featuring a nice, insistent funky groove (it was apparently another attempt at replicating the 'feel' of The Band), it's a charming little composition. The characterful punctuations of electric guitar and piano throughout enliven the song's instrumental backing, which again exudes a slightly loose, 'jam' feel. Meanwhile, vocally, Joey handles the lead well and is ably supported by Tom, who provides the attractive back-up harmonies. Another song from the original, rejected Geoff Emerick-produced album; this still stands as a very decent tune indeed.

This song was eventually released as a bonus track on both the 1992 CD reissue of *No Dice* and the 2010 digital reissue of *Straight Up*.

'Loving You'** (Gibbins)

Finally, we have a Mike Gibbins composition on our hands! Originally given a place on the rejected Geoff Emerick-produced record, this likeable tune features an appealing, waltz-like melody and also boasts a lead vocal from the drummer. There's some nice electric guitar work throughout and Mike's drumming impresses again. Overall, it's a pleasant enough listen, but it was quite rightly replaced by better, later numbers that ultimately appeared on the final *Straight Up* record.

This song was also released as a bonus track on the 1992 CD reissue of *No Dice* and the 2010 digital reissue of *Straight Up*.

'Sing For The Song'** (Evans)

Another Evans composition originally put forward for the suggested, yet ultimately rejected, Geoff Emerick-produced album. It's a catchy, singalong-style tune which starts off as a piano-driven number before strings enter the picture and the sound builds to an epic conclusion whereupon a whole host of voices join in on the 'Sing for the song' choral coda (apparently, anyone who happened to be around in the studio at the time was recruited for this closing singalong). The Beatles' influence heard on the track is, again, not all that surprising given Geoff Emerick's involvement. The addition of strings to the piano foundation, the drum style, the use of flanging – it all bears an easily recognisable resemblance to the later work of the Fab Four but, again, that's not a bad thing – this is, ultimately, a fun, likeable track.

However, as with the previous tracks originally scheduled for the Geoff Emerick-produced LP that was ultimately rejected, I believe better material came along with later producers, George Harrison and Todd Rundgren, and that the resultant *Straight Up* album offered a stronger, more consistent and cohesive collection of songs than the proposed Emerick album.

This song was eventually released as a bonus track on the 2010 CD reissue of the *Straight Up* album.

'Hurry On Father' (Ham)

This strummed, acoustic ballad demo from the period features some lovely, sensitive Pete Ham vocals over a simple yet catchy melody. Very short but very sweet. This home demo is available on Pete's *Golders Green* CD album.

'I'm So Lonely' (Ham)

Another Pete Ham demo from the period, this is a funkier sounding number with a nice, insistent groove. As was quite common with Pete, he manages to combine a fairly positive, toe-tapping melody with opposing 'deep and meaningful' lyrical content, which in this instance concerns a life being lived in the spotlight. This home demo is also available on Pete's *Golders Green* CD.

Ass

Personnel:
Pete Ham: guitar, piano, synthesiser, vocals
Tom Evans: bass, vocals
Joey Molland: guitar, piano, vocals
Mike Gibbins: drums, vocals
Recorded at Apple, Morgan, Air, Trident and Olympic Studios – London, UK and
The Manor, Oxfordshire, UK (various sessions January 1972 – May 1973)
Produced by Chris Thomas and Badfinger, except for * by Todd Rundgren; All
tracks mixed by Chris Thomas and Badfinger; All songs written and arranged by
Badfinger
UK release date: March 1974
US release date: November 1973
Highest chart places: UK: Did not chart, US: 122

By the middle of 1972, Badfinger were riding high on a wave of both critical
acclaim and commercial success. Their last four singles had all been worldwide
hits and their last two albums had also been selling strongly, particularly
in the US. 'Without You', the Ham and Evans-penned track from 1970s *No
Dice* album, had also been covered by Harry Nilsson and hit the number 1
spot in both the US and UK during the first half of 1972. At this juncture, all
the indications were that Badfinger were on the verge of becoming global
superstars, with a realistic future of not only emulating but possibly surpassing
the success of their Apple Records labelmates, the founding fathers themselves,
The Beatles. However, just eighteen months later, dogged by ruinous
misfortune, the dream would be well and truly over. Bad management, legal
wrangling, strained interpersonal relationships, jealousy, infighting, poor
decision-making – and just a plain dose of bad luck – put paid to their chances
of becoming global music titans. It was against this increasingly troubled and
turbulent backdrop that the band created and delivered *Ass*.

Recording sessions actually began as early as January 1972 (at Apple
Studios), with Todd Rundgren still on production duties after the previous
album *Straight Up*. However, Rundgren lasted less than a week and departed
the project due to business disagreements involving production credits.
Apparently, Todd was upset that some of his production revamp work (on the
George Harrison-produced numbers) had not been credited on *Straight Up*
and he hadn't been paid for that work either. He didn't want a repeat of this
situation with *Ass* and tried, unsuccessfully, to negotiate with Apple. Despite
only lasting about a week, two songs were completed during this time – 'The
Winner' and 'I Can Love You'.

After this false start, further recording was put on hold while the band
fulfilled touring commitments (supporting the previous LP, *Straight Up*) from
February through to August. Just before the Summer US tour dates, Joey got
married to Kathie, but it was a less cheery time for another band member –

Mike suddenly announced he was quitting the band! Hurtful criticism and other frustrations had pushed him over the edge and he'd finally had enough. A replacement drummer (Rob Stawinski) was hastily recruited for the tour, but upon the band's return to the UK after the tour had finished, Mike's resolve to leave the band had dissipated somewhat and after some reassuring encouragement from his fellow band members, he returned to the fold in October.

Aside from some rather unproductive recording sessions at Apple Studios (with various session drummers standing in for Mike) in September, work on the album didn't really get going until the following month, after Mike had returned. Now set up in Morgan Studios, the band worked on several numbers, including 'Do You Mind', 'Cowboy', 'Timeless' and 'When I Say'. They had also taken the decision to produce the record themselves, feeling that they would make a better job of it without any external creative interference. It was also at this time that the band signed a new record deal with Warner Brothers (WB), due to take hold the following September (in 1973) just after the Apple contract had expired. The band's business manager, Stan Polley, had seemingly brokered a very financially lucrative deal with WB and since Apple was struggling with many business issues at this time (and only really interested in investing in solo Beatle projects) it was a bit of a no-brainer for the band to sign to WB. As it turned out, *Ass* was the last record released under the Apple label that wasn't by an ex-Beatle.

In November, the band relocated to The Manor recording studio, based in Oxfordshire, UK, where they continued working on the album up until the Christmas/New Year holiday period. Following this short break, the band immediately resumed sessions in January, spending time at both Trident Studios and Air Studios putting the finishing touches to their new album. By mid-January, the band had submitted the completed and mixed album to Apple and then set off on yet another US tour where they performed some of the new album's songs, namely 'Blind Owl' and 'Timeless'.

However, upon their return from the US tour in February, they were greeted with the rather disappointing news that Apple had rejected their album! The truth of the matter was, despite enjoying the creative freedom of producing themselves, the recording sessions had been undisciplined and had quickly become directionless. Various band members later admitted that the sessions at Manor Studios, in particular, had been a little loose and unruly with a generous amount of dope and hash cakes being consumed. Pete Ham also had this to say in a March 1974 interview (an audio excerpt of this hotel interview, conducted on 29 March 1974, was made available on the bonus CD which accompanied the second edition of Dan Matovina's *Without You – The Tragic Story of Badfinger*, released in 2000):

We tried to produce *Ass* ourselves, initially, and we needed somebody to save the day, because we weren't all that experienced at it, you know? Well, the thing is, everybody hears it differently? I mean, everybody's idea of a good production is different, you know, and that was one of the problems with the group trying to produce itself because we had four different opinions ... (so) we just had to get somebody from the outside with that ear to say 'Hold it. You've gone a bit nuts there. Let's just do it like this'. I think there is a need for good producers.

Therefore, to help salvage the album, Apple chose Chris Thomas as the man for the job. The band readily approved of Chris as they had liked his previous production work with bands such as Procol Harum. Chris had also worked on The Beatles' *White Album,* which hadn't done his street cred any harm either.

So, in early April 1973, the band headed back to the studio, this time to Olympic Studios in London. With Chris Thomas at the production helm, the band carried out restoration work on several songs as well as working on new material such as 'Constitution' and 'Icicles'. By mid-May, a newly spruced up and rejuvenated album was presented to Apple, which was duly accepted. However, if the band thought that all was now well, they were slowly to realise that things were actually only going to get worse. Expecting a summer release for the new album, further delays ensued, due not only to the forthcoming changeover from Apple to WB but also because of a major Joey Molland-related copyright issue. When Joey had joined Badfinger, he had not signed the original Apple publishing agreement. He subsequently signed over individual song copyrights as each album was completed. However, with *Ass*, Stan Polley refused to turn over Joey's copyrights to Apple until certain business demands had been met, hence the further delay in releasing the album.

The album title *Ass* was Tom Evans' idea and was intended to reflect his feelings about what was happening to the group at that time (humorously namechecking their previous album titles) – 'No Dice, Straight Up your Ass!' The cover artwork, too, was intended to mirror the group's feelings with regards to transitioning from Apple to WB – a picture of a giant, God-like hand high up in the heaven's proffering a giant carrot down to a lowly donkey down on Earth – subtle it ain't!

Finally, in November 1973, two years after their last album had come out, *Ass* was released, at least in the US. The UK release was delayed even further, eventually arriving in record stores during March 1974. Disappointingly, however, the releases in both countries arrived with little fanfare and virtually zero promotion. It would seem that the old adages 'out of sight, out of mind' and, indeed, 'time and tide wait for no man' hold true in this case, and what with Apple's complete lack of interest in marketing and promoting the album, *Ass* didn't really stand a chance. Reviews were also, unsurprisingly, few and far between and mixed at best. Some of the more positive reviews focused on their achievement of attaining a more distinctive sound and identity on the new album. *Billboard* had this to say:

A very well-done set from this vastly overlooked British band. Their fusion of strong vocal harmony with both intricate acoustic guitar work and a straight rock sound give them the combination that should attract overdue attention. Previously thought of as mere Beatles sound-alikes, this foursome displays its own musical style with cuts like 'When I Say' and 'Blind Owl'.

Rolling Stone concurred:

...they've discovered their own identity as a group, and that discovery gives this album its surprising forcefulness ... The album consists almost entirely of bracing rock & roll, snarling and snapping at the choirboy vocals hovering just above ... the most viable self-representation Badfinger has yet recorded ... This is a surprisingly vibrant album from a group that has never managed to string its scattered hits into a distinguishable identity ... It would qualify as a comeback if it weren't so clearly an introduction to the band beneath the veneer.

The review of the album published in *Cash Box* was also in accordance with this sentiment:

The British band that has sounded so much like the Beatles on some of its records is really establishing an individualistic style on its latest LP ... Naturally, the quintessence of harmonic perfection is resplendent on several of the cuts ... the experience they've garnered from their past efforts is in full evidence here.

There were, of course, just as many negative reviews which really stuck the knife in. *Circus* magazine described *Ass* as 'another self-explanatory LP from a once inspired band that has since drifted into the rock valley of fatigue' whilst concluding that 'Another LP like this and these boys will be making a living playing in sleezoid Long Island bars'. The UK music press were also generally pretty derogatory and disparaging in their assessments of the new record. *Melody Maker*: 'The first side is directionless and material is poor ... the major part of each track is emotionless and spineless.' However, their review went on to begrudgingly concede that the flip side of the record was an improvement, with the best track being 'Timeless', which the magazine described as 'a high, wide and really quite handsome production job'. The *NME*, meanwhile, pulled no punches at all in its review of the new album, stating that '...the choice of material is dismally devoid of inspiration ... *Ass* is deadly dull.' Even more retrospective assessments have refused to re-evaluate this particular album in a more positive light. Stephen Thomas Erlewine, in his online *AllMusic* review, states that '*Ass* is the sound of a pop band rocking out rather clumsily ... a misguided effort, heavy on stumbling rockers and mediocre songs.'

Given the somewhat muted critical response upon release, it's perhaps unsurprising that the album only stuttered to #122 in the US *Billboard* 200 chart. In the UK, it fared even worse and sank without even bothering the charts at all.

In my opinion, *Ass* is probably the band's most overlooked and undervalued album – not just by music critics but often the fans too. To be honest, my first reaction upon hearing *Ass* echoed the general critical consensus that the album was below par and a disappointment after previous efforts. I initially felt that there was an overabundance of mediocre, workmanlike rockers and ballads. And why so many Joey Molland tracks – half the album was dominated by Joey's tracks; and no offence, I respected and appreciated Joey's talents, but where was Pete on this album – and to a slightly lesser extent – where was Tom? It all just seemed a bit bland – pleasant but unmemorable and, 'Apple Of My Eye' aside, lacking any real classics. However, I have since revisited this album many, many times and each subsequent listen results in proving my initial thoughts entirely erroneous. More and more, I have come to appreciate it's maybe less than obvious charms but, to use a well-worn cliché, this album is most definitely 'a grower'. *Ass* is the sound of a band finally feeling relaxed and confident enough to realise its true potential and they ultimately ended up delivering a great, harmonious piece of work full of hidden treasures.

Ass was first released on CD in 1996 (with an additional bonus track) and then reissued again in 2010 as part of Apple Records' major album reissue campaign (with additional bonus tracks).

'Apple Of My Eye' (Ham)

Released as a single A-side (b/w 'Blind Owl'): December 1973 (US), chart #102; March 1974 (UK), did not chart

This is definitely one of the strongest contenders for best track on the album and is the closest thing on *Ass* to the classic power-pop sound of their earlier days. The lyrics are simple and direct and the listener is left in no doubt as to the sentiment of the song. It is Pete's farewell love letter to Apple, a heartfelt goodbye to not only their record label but also their spiritual home. Being so literal, the song could have ended up being incredibly mawkish, but Pete's earnest and sincere vocal delivery wins the listener over. The lyrics are carried along by a wonderfully lilting melody powered by beautiful twin acoustic guitars and backed by gorgeous harmonious vocals.

Oh, I'm sorry but it's time to move away
Though inside my heart I really want to stay
Believe the love we have is so sincere
You know the gift you have will always be

You're the apple of my eye
You're the apple of my heart
But now the time has come to part

One is actually left feeling quite moved after listening to this touching ode to Apple. I mean, how many other songs exist out there which reflect an artist's sadness and regret at leaving their record label – I can't think of any!

An 'early mix' version of the song (produced by the band themselves) was released on the 2010 CD reissue as a bonus track.

'Get Away' (Molland)

The first of Joey's five contributions to the album, this song is a solid little boogie rocker. Joey's vocals are terrific and it was on this track that he was actually recorded playing piano for the first time. Pete also shines with some extremely confident lead guitar. As for the sentiment of the piece, Joey actually wrote the song in response to Pete and his renowned devotion and dedication to songwriting and this is particularly highlighted in the first verse of the song (Joey's attitude to work seemingly tended to be a little more relaxed!):

> You may be right, working all night and day
> But I know sometimes I've got to get away

An 'alternative' version of the song (produced by the band themselves) was released on the 2010 digital reissue as a bonus track.

'Icicles' (Molland)

Another Joey-penned track, this was one of the new songs first worked on with Chris Thomas in the producer's chair. The catchy ballad kicks off with a lovely bit of backward electric guitar before Joey's vocals kick in. A captivating melody soon takes hold and is enhanced by some great electric guitar work throughout and, in particular, there is a nice little guitar solo halfway through courtesy of Pete. This song was performed live in concert for the BBC and recorded at the Paris Theatre, London, on 10 August 1973 (and is available on the *Badfinger - BBC In Concert 1972-3* CD).

'The Winner'* (Molland)

Another snappy and appealing Molland-composed mid-tempo rocker, this track is driven along wonderfully by Pete's insistent buzzing guitar. The lyrics, meanwhile, take a swipe at a certain Apple labelmate:

> You can drive a car, be a movie star, any day of the week
> You don't have to shout, or walk about, you just have to speak...
> ...Here he comes, that's a winner
> Here he come, take a look, write a book

Joey discussed the sentiment of the song in the Cimino-authored biography:

> I wrote this song about John Lennon. I was really angry with him. I was really pissed off because it seemed like everything I read in the paper, he was always

moaning. He was bitching about everything. Every single thing. There were
no good things in this guy's life. Just amazing. What the fuck, you know? So, I
wrote this song.

The song concludes with the rest of the band contributing to a lovely,
harmonious vocal chant on the fade out – 'Yeah, we all understand.' Sublime.

An 'alternative' version of the song (produced by the band themselves) was
released on the 2010 digital reissue as a bonus track.

'Blind Owl' (Evans)
The first Tom Evans-penned track on the album finds the musician meditating
on the band's experiences on the road.

Pill-driven skills, weeping whippoorwills
Too much going round to get high…
…Days, plays, interviewer's maze
Play the role, sell your soul
Becoming to yourself
A hero who must never lie

It's a superb toe-tapper of a piece that boogies along nicely. As usual, there
is great guitar work throughout, backing Tom's well-delivered musings on
touring. Towards the end of the song, massed band vocals begin to chant, 'Who
has never lied! Who has never lied!' backed by a charming cowbell, culminating
in a searing guitar solo courtesy of Pete.

This track was performed live during 1973-74 and well-performed live
versions can be found on both the *Badfinger – BBC In Concert 1972-3* CD and
also the *Day After Day – Badfinger Live* album.

An 'alternative' version of the song (produced by the band themselves) was
released on the 2010 CD reissue as a bonus track. Tom's acoustic guitar demo
version, offering an embryonic take on the song, was also made available
on the bonus CD that accompanied the second edition of the Matovina
biography.

'Constitution' (Molland)
This is arguably Joey's best track on the album. 'Constitution' is a stonking,
blues-style rocker which veers towards Hendrix and Cream territory with its
heavy sounding riff. Pete's incendiary lead guitar is riveting and it's no wonder
that this rifftastic tune became one of Badfinger's live staples.

Indeed, songs like this and 'Blind Owl' show off the band's live boogie rock
direction. Up to this point in time, Badfinger 'live' had been a completely
different beast to the studio version of the band. When live, they tended to
perform more boogie/blues rock/jamming and covers than power-pop and
their own hit singles. This was probably due to them rebelling against the

Above: The classic line-up in its prime, from left to right: Joey Molland (seated), Mike Gibbins, Tom Evans and Pete Ham. (*Pictorial Press Ltd/Alamy Stock Photo*)

MAYBE TOMORROW
IVEYS

Left: The fresh-faced
foursome in their pre-
Badfinger guise The Iveys.
They are all smiles for the
cover of their debut album.
(*Apple Records*)

MAGIC CHRISTIAN MUSIC
•BY
BADfINGER

Right: The debut album
from the newly rechristened
Badfinger. (*Apple Records*)

BADfINGER

APPLE 20

COME AND GET IT

Left: The short-lived trio
(post-Ron/pre-Joey) invite
listeners to 'Come And Get It'
on the debut Badfinger single.
(*Apple Records*)

Right: The 1969 satirical black comedy film *The Magic Christian* starring Peter Sellers and Ringo Starr, featured specially commissioned music by Badfinger. (*Commonwealth United*)

Below: Whilst the film itself was criticised, the accompanying original soundtrack album was well-received. (*Commonwealth United Records*)

The Magic Christian is: antiestablishmentarian, antibellum, antitrust, antiseptic, antibiotic, antisocial, & antipasto.

Above: 'Carry On Till Tomorrow' plays over the film's opening titles. (*Commonwealth United*)

Left: The Iveys in action, shooting a promo film for the 'Maybe Tomorrow' single. (*Apple Records*)

Right: A baby-faced Mike demonstrates intense concentration during the shoot. (*Apple Records*)

Left: The rather dapper looking and besuited boys filmed the promo clip in the Apple Basement Studio at 3 Savile Row early in 1969. (*Apple Records*)

Right: The boys enjoying themselves on German TV (*Beat-Club*), promoting 'Come And Get It' early in 1970.

Left: The rather hirsute Joey and Tom, performing their debut global smash hit.

Right: Pete tinkling the ivories during the *Beat-Club* performance.

Left: The front cover of *No Dice*, the band's highest-charting album in the US. (*Apple Records*)

Right: 'No Matter What' is ranked number one on *VH1*'s '20 Essential Power Pop Tracks That Will Be Stuck In Your Head Forever'. (*Apple Records*)

Left: *Straight Up*, a record that David Fricke (of *Rolling Stone* magazine) later called their 'power-pop apex'. (*Apple Records*)

Right: The band's final album for Apple, *Ass*, is possibly the group's most underrated work. (*Apple Records*)

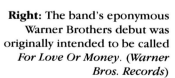

Left: 'Apple of my Eye', Pete's fond farewell to the Apple label. (*Apple Records*)

Right: The band's eponymous Warner Brothers debut was originally intended to be called *For Love Or Money*. (*Warner Bros. Records*)

Left: Pete giving it his all during a *Top of the Pops* TV performance of 'No Matter What' in early 1971.

Right: The band performing their global Top Ten smash hit, 'No Matter What', for the prestigious *Top of the Pops* TV show.

Left: The band performing 'Day After Day' on TV in 1972.

Right: Pete in action, singing 'Day After Day' on Granada TV, 1972.

Left: The band performing 'Without You' on TV in 1972.

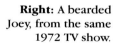

Right: A bearded Joey, from the same 1972 TV show.

Left: The band performing 'Baby Blue' on Canadian TV in 1972.

Right: Tom lends his emotive backing vocals to 'Baby Blue', their last major hit single.

Left: Pete's 'Baby Blue' experienced a resurgence in popularity in 2013 when the song featured in the finale of TV series *Breaking Bad*.

Right: *Wish You Were Here*. Possibly the band's greatest album and could have been a hit if it hadn't been pulled from stores! (*Warner Bros. Records*)

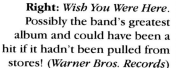

Left: The back cover of *Wish You Were Here*. Sadly, this was the last album to be released by the classic line-up of Pete, Tom, Joey and Mike. (*Warner Bros. Records*)

Right: The *Head First* record finally saw the light of day when *Snapper Music* released the rough mixes nearly 26 years after recording! (*Snapper Music*)

Left: Joey and Tom are back on the *Airwaves*! (*Elektra Records*)

Right: A lovely shot of Joey and Tom from the *Airwaves* record cover. (*Elektra Records*)

Left: Peter Max's distinctive cover art for the *Say No More* LP. (*Radio Records, Inc./Real Music/ Gonzo Multimedia*)

Right: Tom and Joey, taken from the 'Love Is Gonna Come At Last' promo film. (*Elektra Records*)

Left: 'Love Is Gonna Come At Last' peaked at #69 on the *Billboard* chart during April 1979. (*Elektra Records*)

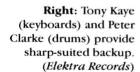

Right: Tony Kaye (keyboards) and Peter Clarke (drums) provide sharp-suited backup. (*Elektra Records*)

Left: Badfinger recorded two seven-song shows, in 1972 and 1973 respectively, for broadcast on the BBC. (*Strange Fruit Ltd*)

Right: Released in 2021, *The Lost Broadcasts* album features a number of rare BBC Radio session tracks by both The Iveys and Badfinger. (*Cantare*)

Left: The much-maligned 'live' album, *Day After Day* released in 1990. (*Rykodisc*)

Right: *Timeless... The Musical Legacy* was released in the wake of Badfinger's resurgence in popularity due to the inclusion of 'Baby Blue' in the *Breaking Bad* TV series finale. (*Apple Corps Ltd.*)

Left: The boys taking some time out during recording on the *Timeless* cover. (*Apple Corps Ltd.*)

Right: Joey Molland and assorted famous friends revisited the band's musical history in 2021. (*Cleopatra Records, Inc.*)

Steve Wozny   Mark Healey   Joey Molland   Mike Ricciardi

Joey
Molland's
BAD f INGER

Above: Joey Molland continues to fly the flag for Badfinger in the 21st century with his touring version of the band. (*Joey Molland*)

Above: Bob Jackson started touring with his version of Badfinger in 2015. (*Bob Jackson/BadfingerUK*)

'lightweight pop act' tag that had seemingly been bestowed upon them by the press at the time (mainly the UK press, it has to be said) but was also driven by the fact that it was harder to reproduce some of their more intricate numbers in a live setting due to their limited on-stage instrumentation. This, in turn, ultimately influenced the overall sound of *Ass*. Pete, again from that March 1974 hotel interview, explained that they were trying to get more of that live feel and on-stage group togetherness into the songs rather than produce a studio album with too much overdubbing on it. Hence, this album finds the band branching out into an overall, harder-edged boogie rock sound infiltrated by a touch of blues 'n' country.

Dynamic live versions of this track can be found on both the *Badfinger – BBC In Concert 1972-3* CD and also the *Day After Day – Badfinger Live* album.

'When I Say' (Evans)

Written after a brief falling out with his then-girlfriend, Marianne (they eventually got married in May 1973), Tom was definitely from that breed of songwriters who need some form of intense emotional stimulation to help them compose lyrics. Indeed, this was essentially confirmed later on by Marianne herself (in the Matovina biography), when she revealed that Tom had told her it was easier for him to write when he was depressed. Whatever the inspiration, 'When I Say' is an appealing ballad which opens with a sparkling acoustic arrangement and builds gradually, through added layers of sound, to a soaring peak of twin lead guitars. Lyrically, it is a simple, honest and direct love song to Marianne, and it is convincingly presented by Tom, who delivers an impressively earnest and impassioned lead vocal:

> I'm not the one who'll give you everything you need
> But what I mean is that I'll try
> I can't deny that I've been burning inside
> For all the things I'll never see
> So come on, be yourself, nothing else
> Who could ask for any more?

Tom, not surprisingly, later cited it as one of his favourite personal compositions.

An 'alternative' version of the song (produced by the band themselves) was released on the 2010 digital reissue as a bonus track.

'Cowboy' (Gibbins)

With Mike Gibbins' first penned track on the album, we are treated to a complete change of pace. A faux country tune inspired by Mike's watching of a Western/cowboy movie, it's a lovely, fun song, albeit slightly bonkers! Personally, I find the track utterly charming and it definitely provides some light relief from the rest of the solemn soul-searching found elsewhere on the album. A delightful wobble-board effect runs throughout the song, punctuated by bursts of harmonica and fiddle.

This is most definitely the album's 'Ringo' track, but I find it absolutely irresistible!

'I Can Love You'* (Molland)

A beautiful, sweet acoustic strum opens up this rather lovely sounding Joey Molland ballad, presumably inspired by his (then) soon-to-be wife, Kathie. Carried along on a gentle, melodious wave, the song's sentiment is never overly cloying and reassures us all that everything will turn out alright given time. The only slight drawback is the vocal quality. Joey's delivery, whilst heartfelt, does suffer from some wavering pitch issues. However, this modest quibble aside, the song remains rather enchanting. According to Joey himself (as relayed in the Cimino biography): 'This is the best sounding load of rubbish that I ever wrote!'

An 'alternative' version of the song (produced by the band themselves) was released on the 2010 digital reissue as a bonus track.

'Timeless' (Ham)

Although Pete Ham only ended up contributing two songs to the album, they are both probably the strongest and most memorable tracks on *Ass*. This eight-minute album ending epic starts slowly with strummed guitar and pan flute accompanying Pete's haunted vocals before drums and backing vocal harmonies start adding muscle to the song. A blistering, Harrison-esque, psychedelic-blues guitar solo is then injected into the mix and the whole thing builds to a three-minute, white noise-filled jamming coda, clearly indebted to The Beatles' 'I Want You (She's So Heavy)', before concluding with a single sustained chord (producer Chris Thomas later conceded [in an online Bill Kopp-authored *Record Collector* article from November 2018] that there were indeed similarities in the arrangements of the two songs: 'It's pretty obviously a case of plagiarism!').

As for the theme of the song, Pete's lyrics are quite introspective and philosophically contemplative:

We are yesterday, we are today
We are tomorrow, we are timeless
We are then, we are now
We are the future, we are timeless
We are the sorrow, we are the pain
We are the sunshine, we are the rain
We are love, we are hate
We are the future, we are timeless

The song was performed live throughout 1973-74 (and was allegedly more a case of 'endless' rather than 'timeless' as it was transformed into an extended jam-athon!) and a 'live' version can be found on the *Day After Day – Badfinger Live* CD.

An 'alternative' version of the song (produced by the band themselves) was released on the 2010 CD reissue as a bonus track.

Other Contemporary Songs
'Do You Mind' (Molland)

A good, solid, mid-tempo number from Joey enhanced by some lovely slide guitar work throughout. The lyrics are quite subtle and the specific message of the song is a little inconspicuous, but it's certainly a pleasant enough listen. Aside from the two Rundgren-produced tracks from early 1972, this was the first *Ass* track worked on when recording began in earnest in October 1972. This track was on the original album submitted to Apple in January 1973 but was later removed from the tracklisting when the album was re-jigged and resubmitted in May of that year.

Two different versions of the song (both produced by the band themselves) have been released on the 1996 and 2010 CD reissues, respectively, as bonus tracks.

'Regular' (Molland)

This track is essentially performed as a good old English pub singalong. It is sung by Joey in an inebriated style and ends with some equally intoxicated-sounding honky-tonk piano. By all accounts, Joey drank half a bottle of whiskey to sing it and was indeed very drunk – nothing wrong with a bit of method acting!

As with 'Do You Mind', this track was on the original album submission in January 1973. In all honesty, although it is indeed a fun track, it was probably the right decision to remove it from the revised track listing.

This song (produced by the band themselves) was released on the 2010 CD reissue as a bonus track.

'Piano Red' (Ham)

This is basically a honky-tonk blues parody. Pete and the band sound like they're having tremendous fun recording this and it is indeed a joy to hear the track. It's one of those songs where your feet start tapping, your head starts nodding and a great big smile breaks out on your face. This was another track on the original album track listing but was later removed when the album was being revised.

As with 'Regular', it's another joyful and entertaining listen and, indeed, most unlike their usual output. However, I'm once again not altogether surprised that this one got pulled later as well. One could even possibly accuse the band of a certain degree of self-indulgency during their self-produced sessions! Although some fans may, therefore, question why Mike's 'Cowboy' was left on the album while these other 'lighter' songs were removed. Well ... it may be that everyone involved in the track listing decision-making process felt that the album needed just the one lighter moment and perhaps chose Mike's tune over the others so that he actually had some discernible presence on the album (not to belittle Mike's solid drumming at all, it's just that it's overshadowed somewhat by the quality of Pete's songs and guitar playing, Joey's prolific song output and even Tom's modest offerings).

This song (produced by the band themselves) was released on the 2010 digital reissue as a bonus track whilst a solo demo version (featuring Pete on piano and slide acoustic guitar) can be found as a bonus track on the Japanese edition of Pete's *Golders Green* album.

'Dreaming' (Molland)
Another quality blues-style rocker from Joey containing some great lead guitar and harmonica work by Pete. I'm really not sure why it wasn't considered for any version of the album back in 1973, nor why it hasn't been included as a bonus track on any reissue since – a real mystery!

'Rock 'N' Roll' (Evans)
Another great rocker this one, courtesy of Tom Evans. There is some inspired guitar work throughout and great piano playing, but it is another mysterious omission from any version of the album either submitted (in 1973), released or subsequently reissued! It's a real shame because Tom, despite ending up with two tracks on the final release, still feels a little anonymous on this album next to Pete and Joey. The addition of this rather fine track would certainly have redressed that situation and added more balance to the album.

Allegedly, a few weeks prior to the 1996 CD reissue of the album, a few Abbey Road Studios-mastered C90 cassettes of *Ass* were distributed to a handful of music industry people. It appears from the track listing on these cassettes that *Ass* was originally planned to have five bonus tracks: 'Dreaming', 'Piano Red', 'Rock 'N' Roll', 'Regular' and 'Do You Mind'. However, this idea was clearly scrapped as 'Do You Mind', as noted above, was the only one included on the 1996 CD release. 'Piano Red' and 'Regular' were, as previously noted, eventually issued on the 2010 CD/digital reissues, but that still leaves 'Dreaming' and 'Rock 'N' Roll' without an official release. Let's keep our fingers crossed that they will one day make an official appearance – they're simply too good to keep locked away.

'Coppertone Blues' (Ham)
A beautiful, stately, melodic ballad from the pen of Pete Ham. Regarding the lyrical content, *Coppertone* is a well-known US brand of sunscreen, so perhaps this is an ode to a girlfriend who used to use it, or perhaps Pete was merely inspired by the model who appeared in *Coppertone* advertising. Either way, it's an enticing tune and one which was considered as a possible album contender as an instrumental backing track was produced during the *Ass* sessions. This backing track outtake has been made available on various bootlegs over the years, whilst the Pete Ham solo demo version was released on Pete's 7 *Park Avenue* album.

'Richard' (Ham)

This composition is a real oddity in the Pete Ham song catalogue. Written as an ode to a man's private parts, this cheeky little number reveals a rather different (and naughty) side to Pete. It's actually rather refreshing to hear Pete having fun on this tune. Lively and fun, this amusing rocker offers an appealing change of mood from the composer. Pete also delivers some pretty nifty harmonica work too. This home demo can be found on Pete's *Golders Green* album.

'I've Waited So Long To Be Free' (Ham)

This Ham-penned demo from the period sees the writer return to more familiar territory. Featuring downhearted lyrics delivered by a suitably world-weary vocal, this song does, however, stand out for its unusual use of a four-letter word! This home demo is also available on Pete's *Golders Green* album.

'Whiskey Man' (Ham)

Another Ham-penned demo from around 1972, this one serves as a convincing blues pastiche. Short and sweet, this tune also boasts some fine harmonica work from Pete. This home demo is another track that can be found on Pete's *Golders Green* album.

'A Lonely Day' (Ham)

Yet another home demo from the incredibly prolific Pete Ham. Written circa 1972 again, the light and poppy tune presented by the composer juxtaposes nicely with the deeper and more emotional lyrical content. This home demo can also be found on Pete's *Golders Green* CD.

'You're Such A Good Woman' (Ham)

A further 1972 home demo by Pete. This one, a rather earnest ballad, was not released on either of Pete's home demo CD collections but did later appear as the B-side to a very limited-edition vinyl single (500 copies) issued in 2013 on the Without You Music label (the A-side was a 1975 Pete Ham home demo called 'No, Don't Let It Go').

'Miss Misunderstood' (Molland)

This one's a Joey Molland-penned song demo from the *Ass* period. Two distinct home demo versions (one acoustic, the other electric) are available on Joey's *Demo's Old and New* CD (Gonzo Multimedia, 2015). It's really impressive just how prolific Joey was during this period, but more than that, the quality of his songwriting at this time is also of such a high standard. He really was getting into his stride during the *Ass* period and his growing confidence as a songwriter is well and truly reflected in his songs from this era.

As for this particular track, 'Miss Misunderstood', the lyrics clearly show Joey standing up for his new wife. Much like Yoko's relationship with the other Beatles, Kathie Molland also had a somewhat strained relationship at times with Joey's bandmates. Joey defends his wife valiantly on this track and although only available in home demo form, this certainly has the makings of another thoroughly decent tune. However, given the lyrical intent and the fact that it was never given a full-band studio run through, I'm not sure it was ever seriously considered for the *Ass* album. Maybe it was just a means by which Joey could vent some steam and get something of his chest!

Badfinger

Personnel:
Pete Ham: vocals, guitar, keyboards
Tom Evans: vocals, bass
Joey Molland: vocals, guitar
Mike Gibbins: vocals, drums
Pans by Russ & The Flames; Horns arranged by Jim Horn
Recorded at Olympic Studios, London, UK (June – November 1973); Mixed at Air and Olympic Studios, London, UK
Produced by Chris Thomas
Release date: February 1974
Highest chart places: UK: Did not chart, US: 161

With the release of *Ass* being temporarily delayed and all associated touring plans cancelled, the band were instructed by their management to commence recording sessions for their debut WB album. Justifiably, the band were not at all happy with this situation. They were understandably worn out and since only several weeks had passed since the conclusion of the *Ass* sessions, they were also lacking in new material. However, despite feeling dejected at the delayed release of *Ass* and the subsequent cancellation of all supporting gigs, the band reluctantly acquiesced to their management's demands and duly entered Olympic Studios in June 1973, with Chris Thomas once again sitting in the producer's chair.

Chris Thomas later recalled (in a 2019 interview with *CultureSonar*) that the prevailing mood within the band at this juncture was most definitely not a happy one:

> We had to make another album very shortly after *Ass*, something crazy like six weeks later. They were non-plussed about it all, a very bizarre situation. They had an American manager called Stan Polley, and the band was losing money. So then we made another album.

So, despite lacking any real motivation, the band commenced work on the new album. Session productivity, perhaps unsurprisingly given the band's mood at that time, proved rather sluggish and it wasn't until November that the recording sessions came to a belated conclusion. As the project had dragged on, so the band's interest had begun to wane and, by the end, everyone was exhausted. Not everyone was convinced by the overall quality of the final product either. Joey Molland expressed his rather honest thoughts in Dan Matovina's band biography:

> That was the first time we had what I thought were weak tracks. Up to that point, I had liked everything we did. Also, we were pissed off about the management, and I think it affected the recording adversely.

Chris Thomas also later questioned his own project input in the Matovina tome:

> They were definitely getting discouraged and depressed. But much of what happened with that album was partly my fault. I was experimenting a lot, trying different approaches from one song to the next. I don't know if it was particularly the right thing to do.

Before the album was even completed, a single was released in the UK only. One of the first tracks worked on, Joey's 'Love Is Easy' was issued as a single in October 1973. Bizarrely, this single ended up appearing in the shops several months before their final Apple output had even been released (the 'Apple of my Eye' single appeared in February 1974 whilst the *Ass* album wasn't in the shops until March in the UK)! Not the most obvious choice for a single, the UK music press at the time generally regarded it with indifference and, subsequently, it completely flopped upon release. The single's lack of success, of course, did nothing to improve the band's humour at this time.

As for the debut WB album itself, the original December 1973 release date had to be scrapped due to the delayed release of *Ass* and it wasn't released globally until February 1974 (in the UK, the whole messy Apple/WB album release schedule situation was even worse as the WB debut actually ended up being released just a few weeks ahead of *Ass* which undoubtedly hurt both albums commercially due to the utter confusion caused. Indeed, Joey Molland was particularly scathing in his assessment of the situation when interviewed for VH1's *Behind the Music* in 2000: 'It was a stupid thing to do. You don't put two records out at the same time and, you know, fight yourself. You're fighting everybody else!'). When the album did finally appear in the shops, it did so with the eponymous title *Badfinger*. However, this had not been the intended album title. Originally, Tom Evans had come up with the suggestion *For Love Or Money,* which was, of course, a fairly explicit reference to their dilemma over having signed the lucrative WB record deal. The band was apparently quite surprised when the title was subsequently changed and Pete Ham was later reported as saying that WB were not happy with their title proposal and took it upon themselves to amend it. Apparently, the band had no say in the album cover design either (the front cover of the record ended up being an image of a seemingly well-to-do woman, decked out in equestrian attire, posing with a cigarette holder, whilst the back cover was a photograph of the band members astride horses). Joey Molland had this to say in an October 1981 interview with *Goldmine* magazine when asked why the originally intended album title hadn't been used:

> Because the album that we wanted to do was like a postcard album. It was too expensive and Warners wouldn't go along with it. It was like a double album cover, and the front of it was just a single leaf and it would have had six

postcards on it, with the band logo, and they would have been detachable, so people could have mailed them to their friends. So they didn't want to do it. We found ourselves with an album coming out in two weeks and no album cover. So we quickly went down, outside London, and they hired John Kosh, and we went outside, we got some horses, went for a bit, and he took a photo.

In support of the album, the band undertook their sixth US tour, beginning in February 1974. However, despite the supporting tour and a March US single release (Pete's 'I Miss You'), the band's commercial fortunes failed to improve. The album struggled to 161 in the *Billboard* charts and the accompanying single bombed completely. Regarding the choice of single, not all of the band members were happy with WB's selection. Joey vented his feelings in Michael Cimino's biography:

[Pete] played everything himself. We all thought it was a bit Walt Disney ... Of course, Warner Brothers picked this for the first single in America ... Does that sound like a Badfinger single to you? It had nothing to do with us, other than it was Pete's song. Well, they just told us they were putting it out. I was really angry about it. I was enraged. I told them they shouldn't have put it on the record. I said, 'It's not a Badfinger record. It's a Peter Ham record.' I was outraged.

Reviews for the album itself were mixed as usual. *Rolling Stone* were severely critical of the album:

Pete Ham still writes like Paul McCartney, still plays guitar like George Harrison and still is in dogged pursuit of the Big Ballad – but nothing here approaches the sweep of 'Timeless' on *Ass*. Too often on *Badfinger*, Ham is merely cloying ... the first task confronting Badfinger is to learn how to rock. The up-tempo tracks on *Badfinger* are singularly flat-footed and provide an insufficient contrast to the occasional plod of Ham's ballads. To become a really first-rate band, Badfinger has a long way to go and this album doesn't even begin.

Unfortunately, *Rolling Stone* was not alone in its scathing appraisal of the new album. *Zoo World* condemned what they perceived as the band's new direction and labelled tracks such as 'Matted Spam' and 'My Heart Goes Out' as 'outright crappy tunes'! *Creem* opined that the band had 'run into a crisis' and that 'they want to break away from the Beatles-copyists label, but they don't know where to run'. The *NME* continued its traditional lambasting of the band:

Badfinger have always come out of the studios sounding like a poor man's Beatles ... Unsurprisingly enough, the Beatle influence is clearly evident here ... The tunes are the weakest facet of this record. They show a serious lack of originality and Chris Thomas's too tight production doesn't help either ...

Other British bands have been able to take what are essentially Beatle ideas and make something of them which is quickly identifiable as their own sound ... Badfinger hasn't pulled it off.

Thankfully, there were other contemporary music periodicals that demonstrated far better taste! *Cash Box*: 'This collection, their first for their new label, is another great excursion for the group and one that will certainly bring them back into the prominence their talent so richly deserves.' *Record Mirror*'s review headline simply proclaimed 'Stunning 'Finger' whilst their review concluded with the following very wise words: 'It's about time the public realised what a fine band we've got in our midst and latch on to them quickly'. *Billboard* identified Pete Ham as 'one of the finest writers in pop music' and the band as 'one of the most enjoyable congregations around'. *Circus* proclaimed that the band had 'recorded one of the finest albums of their Beatlesque career' whilst *Sounds* echoed these sentiments: 'Every song on this platter is good ... The main basis of this album is sheer melody which makes it so damn good to listen to'. However, because the *Ass* and *Badfinger* albums had been released so closely, they were also sometimes reviewed simultaneously. *Zoo World*:

> Badfinger seemed, at one time, to be the hope of the future for those who relished the past efforts of The Beatles ... Apparently, something has shaken them off their confident path ... These two albums are half-worthy of the Badfinger talent, and it's pretty upsetting.

Meanwhile, *Phonograph Record* had this to say:

> Two Badfinger albums in one month! What more could a fan ask for after a two-year drought? ... actually, the fans will be asking plenty, and Badfinger has a lot to answer for, because these two mediocre albums are already one of the biggest disappointments of the new year.

Retrospective assessments of this album also tend to regard the album with caution. *AllMusic*, for example, had this to say: '*Badfinger* is a bit of a mess. Some moments work quite well ... but they're surrounded with failed experiments and songs that, for one reason or another, just don't click'. Their review concludes by stating that:

> On the whole, *Badfinger* is a stronger record than its immediate predecessor, since it plays to their pop strengths, but there are enough missed opportunities and forgettable moments to make it worthwhile only for truly dedicated fans.

Once the US tour had ended, at the beginning of April 1974, that was pretty much it for the album's promotion. Rather strangely, since the WB record

deal stated that there should be a minimum of three singles per year, no
further singles were released from the record in either the US or UK. I think
it's fair to say that this debut album for WB was handled incredibly poorly by
the label and suffered commercially as a result. This is a real shame because
there are many gems to be found on the record. The first half of the album is
very strong, in my opinion, and despite sagging a little in quality just after the
midway mark, the concluding trio of tunes ensures that the album ends on an
appropriately high note. Producer Chris Thomas revealed his feelings about the
record in his 2019 interview with *CultureSonar*:

> There's not much cohesion to that album, not a lot of direction. I like some of
> it. [But] It didn't get publicised like they wanted.

This album was issued on CD for the first time in the 1990s, followed by
further reissues in the 2000s. The latest 'Expanded Edition' was released in
2018 on the Real Gone Music label with added bonus tracks.

'I Miss You' (Ham)
Released as a single A-side (b/w 'Shine On'): March 1974 (US), did not chart
A beautiful, sweet-sounding, keyboard-based ballad, Pete originally wrote this
tune back in 1968 for his girlfriend of the time. Strong echoes of McCartney
abound throughout this finely crafted romantic ode which was chosen as the
first (and, as it turned out, only) single to be released in the US to promote
the self-titled WB debut. A slightly odd choice of single especially given the fact
that it was essentially a Pete Ham solo track since he had played and recorded
all the instruments himself. As mentioned earlier, not all of the band were
enamoured with this choice of single and hints of interpersonal jealousy are
easily perceptible. Joey's following comment from Dan Matovina's book would
seem to bear this out: 'From the band's point of view, we were always being
promoted as Pete Ham's vehicle. There were a lot of other good songs on that
record.' As it turned out, the record flopped anyway and perhaps this resulting
chart failure vindicated the band's feelings at the time.

'Shine On' (Ham, Evans)
A Pete/Tom collaboration, this country rock-tinged number should really have
been promoted to the A-side of the US single rather than hiding away on
the flip side. Written mainly by Pete (about a new girlfriend) but with lyrical
assistance from Tom, this track was tailor-made for the US market. A catchy and
lively acoustic-based tune, this song provides the album with one of its most
memorable and fully realised moments and could have provided the band with
that much-needed chart success.
   A Pete Ham home demo version, albeit only a brief fragment, is available on
Pete's *Golders Green* CD and gives the listener an opportunity to appreciate
the early creative stages of this composition before Tom Evans later helped to

flesh out the song. A 'work in progress' mix of the song was also released on the 2018 Expanded Edition CD reissue as a bonus track.

'Love Is Easy' (Molland)
Released as a single A-side (b/w 'My Heart Goes Out'): October 1973 (UK), did not chart

One of the first songs to be worked on for the album, this Joey number has a very loose and unfinished feel to it. A strong, driving rhythm initially keeps the momentum of this fun, if somewhat slightly chaotic, rocker going for the most part, but it all begins to fall away by the end. Certainly, lyric-wise, the song completely collapses towards the end. Joey recalled the making of the song in the Cimino and Matovina biographies, respectively: 'The song wasn't complete. I'm not even singing words on the end of it, but everybody liked it so much' ... 'I was just going, 'duuuh doo' because I hadn't finished it yet.'

Personally, I think that I would probably concur with producer Chris Thomas' later assessment of the track in that the final mix is a little inefficient, with the drums definitely being too loud overall. Although I would tend to agree that there are definitely some interesting musical ideas going on here, I believe it's all ultimately presented in a slightly messy and frustrating way.

However, although the final, released track does indeed lack a little finesse, one could argue that this simply adds to the charm of the piece and, clearly, the powers that be at WB saw enough potential in the song's catchy riff and appealing pop hook to help convince them to put this out as the first single in the UK. Of course, the band's constant shadow of misfortune continued to haunt them. This time, apparently, BBC Radio immediately complained about some of the record's distortion effects and 'banned' the record. Joey explained the reason for the radio 'ban' in the Cimino biography: 'The record was too loud. They couldn't play it on the radio. The song would freak everything out, so they didn't play it anymore'. Given the fact that there was no discernible airplay, it comes as no surprise that the single bombed.

Somewhat ironically, this song was performed live in concert for the BBC and recorded at the Paris Theatre, London, 10 August 1973, and is available on the *Badfinger – BBC In Concert 1972-3* album. This BBC concert recording, in my humble opinion, provides ample evidence that the song probably worked better in a live environment rather than as a studio effort. Live, the band's committed and purposeful approach adds a whole different dimension to the studio original and offers us a valuable glimpse at the Badfinger concert experience.

'Song For A Lost Friend' (Ham)
Originally titled 'You Had A Dream', this rather lovely Pete Ham-penned pop tune was written about an old girlfriend (indeed, the same girlfriend that had inspired 'I Miss You'). It's a typically classy Ham number with a strong, catchy melody and is a real contender for my personal favourite track from the album.

Pete's strong, emotive vocal delivery is enhanced in the choruses by, firstly, Joey singing harmony with Pete, and then Tom joining in at the end of the choruses to create a beautifully dense harmonious sound. The song climaxes with Pete's terrific lead guitar joining forces with choirboy harmonies to create a majestic wall of sound ending.

A 'work in progress' mix of the song was released on the 2018 Expanded Edition CD reissue as a bonus track.

'Why Don't We Talk' (Evans)

Tom's first effort on the album, this is a great little tune performed vocally in a very Lennon-esque style. Indeed, if 'I Miss You' was Pete doing McCartney, then this is Tom doing his best John vocal impression. The song, a plea to an estranged lover, begins with a snippet of a tape recording made by Tom. Apparently, one day during recording, Tom purchased a Sony tape recorder and was testing it walking back to the studio. With the prevailing experimental mood in the studio, it was deemed a good idea to kick off the finished track with this brief audio extract. However, not everyone in the band was happy with this time-consuming experimentalism. Mike Gibbins, in particular, apparently got increasingly frustrated with the general pace of working and his frustration reportedly peaked with this particular song and the time taken to record it. This may help to explain why Mike's drums sound like cannons throughout the song – perhaps he was pounding the drum skins in pure exasperation!

'Island' (Molland)

Another good, solid effort from Joey, this is very reminiscent of his heavier rockers on the *Ass* album. It's initially a slower-paced rocker that sees more of Mike's skin-pounding propelling the song onto a succinct Joey guitar solo mid-song. The track continues to build, ultimately reaching a blistering guitar climax courtesy of both Joey and Pete (with an added sprinkle of honky-tonk piano right at the end). Regarding the lyrical content, it's a clear-cut romantic love song, delivered by an earnest and assured lead vocal from Joey.

A 'work in progress' mix of the song was released on the 2018 Expanded Edition CD reissue as a bonus track.

'Matted Spam' (Ham)

This is definitely one of the band's most unusual pieces. It is fundamentally an up-tempo blues rocker, but thanks to the addition of a prominent horn arrangement and some funky rhythm guitar courtesy of Joey, the whole thing becomes an exercise in funk 'n' soul. Pete's original demo featured some aggressive rhythm guitar and was presented as more of a blues-based rocker, but in the studio, it was transformed into a funky, horn-laden number.

However, for me, the faux-funk/soul arrangement just doesn't work. I applaud the boys for attempting something different, but for me, it remains a failed experiment. I just feel that the piece works much better simply as a guitar-driven piece *sans* horns. As evidence to support this, I would present the live version of the song featured on the *Badfinger – BBC In Concert 1972-3* album. Recorded at the Paris Theatre, London, on 10 August 1973, this live rendition is a much more palatable version of the song with nary a horn in sight! I would also strongly recommend checking out Pete's original home demo version, which offers a more stripped-down, funky feel which also includes ad-libbed lyrics to the group's biggest US single, 'Day After Day' (available on Pete's 7 *Park Avenue* CD).

Regarding the source of inspiration for this particular song, which cannot easily be deduced from its rather terrible title, it was the same girlfriend who had also inspired Pete to compose 'Shine On'.

A 'work in progress' mix of the song was also released on the 2018 Expanded Edition CD reissue as a bonus track (again, although still boasting a distinctly funky groove, this version surpasses the final, released version for me as it forgoes the horn and sax treatment).

'Where Do We Go From Here?' (Evans)
A mid-tempo, keyboard-based, pop-rock tune, this Evans-penned number provides a pleasant enough listen but is ultimately fairly pedestrian and run-of-the-mill for the band. The only really memorable thing about the track is the steel drum solo that appears mid-way through the song. Interestingly, the pans were provided by a group called Russ & The Flames, who were actually discovered working in a restaurant just around the corner from the recording studio and, in the prevailing climate of studio experimentation, were quickly drafted in to enhance the track. For me, however, this track and the preceding one, 'Matted Spam', provide the nadir of the album but, thankfully, things improve again from here on out.

A 'work in progress' mix of the song was again released on the 2018 Expanded Edition CD reissue as a bonus track.

'My Heart Goes Out' (Gibbins)
Upon a first listen, this Mike Gibbins contribution might seem a tad slight and inconsequential, but if you give this track a chance and devote further attentive listening time to it, you will be rewarded with a very satisfying listening experience indeed. This tune is a definite 'grower.' The song is a very pretty, winsome and folk-tinged ballad featuring two acoustic guitars. However, due to producer Chris Thomas' experimentation with tape delays, the backing track sounds more like a multitude of mandolins which is incredibly effective and results in a beautiful, tinkling sound that pervades the track. Mike's earnest vocal delivery really helps sell the heartache in the song too. For me, this track is a beautifully understated gem.

A 'work in progress' mix of this song is also available on the 2018 Expanded Edition CD reissue as a bonus track.

'Lonely You' (Ham)

Written for one of his female friends at the time who wanted more than a platonic relationship, this Pete Ham track is a truly magical song and really should have been a single. Featuring Pete's lovely warm vocals accompanied by slide guitar and organ and backed by gloriously layered harmonies, this emotional and captivating ballad could have provided the band with that elusive hit song.

When I ask you just to be my friend
I want to lend a hand
But if we get too close, it's sure to end
Oh, can't you understand?
Lonely you, only you

Similar to Pete's 'I Miss You', this gentle ballad with its lilting melody has definite echoes of McCartney and it remains a crime that this exquisite beauty of a song was hidden away as track ten on the album and not even given exposure as a B-side, let alone as an A-side!

A 'work in progress' mix of the song was again made available on the 2018 Expanded Edition CD reissue as a bonus track.

'Give It Up' (Molland)

This Molland-penned rocker is absolutely terrific and is probably Joey's best track on the album. Opening up fairly quietly and restrained, Joey's world-weary vocals, bemoaning a money-grabbing world, are backed by a gentle electric strum. The song then builds slowly but surely before erupting into a chorus of 'Give it up' backed by a tremendous wall of buzzing guitar and harmonious vocal sounds. Joey plays incredible, buzz-saw lead guitar throughout, ably supported by Pete on rhythm guitar. Tom and Pete do the honours on backing vocals.

Regarding the sentiment of the song, Joey had this to say in the Matovina and Cimino biographies, respectively: 'I think it starts off being about the band. The second verse is about the money-hungry people, the young deceivers who play their games' ... '[It's about] Materialism. It's about all the things that were obviously becoming not important. I was realising more and more things that weren't important.'

We learn to wheel and deal and say goodbye
And madness all around us makes for dyin'
Young deceivers soon turn old
And left to die amongst their gold

A great, seven-minute, epic 'live' version of this song (recorded 4 March 1974, at the Agora Club, Cleveland, Ohio) is available on the *Badfinger Live – Day After Day* CD.

A 'work in progress' mix of the song was again released on the 2018 Expanded Edition CD reissue as a bonus track.

'Andy Norris' (Molland, Molland)
Co-written with his wife Kathie (she helped finish off the lyrics), this is a nice, lively and energetic rocker from Joey. Infectiously buoyant with a strong, insistent rock 'n' roll riff, the album comes to a very satisfying conclusion with this loosely arranged, up-tempo toe-tapper and head rocker. This charming little rock 'n' roll number was actually named after a tape operator friend of the band. However, it turned out that Joey got the guy's name wrong – it was actually Morris, not Norris – and, inexplicably, Joey apparently didn't realise this until years later!

A 'work in progress' mix of the song was again made available on the 2018 Expanded Edition CD reissue as a bonus track.

Other Contemporary Songs
'Love My Lady' (Evans)
This unreleased Tom Evans number recorded during the *Badfinger* sessions eventually saw the light of day as a bonus track on the 2018 Expanded Edition CD reissue. With an original working title of 'Oh, Wow!', this moody tune is a rather plodding, bluesy number enlivened only by the sudden appearance of a great, frenetic guitar jam mid-song, but aside from that and some pleasing bursts of background harmonica throughout it's all a little underwhelming and forgettable really, and I can see why it was left off the original album track listing.

'What You're Doin'' (Molland)
A Joey Molland home demo from 1973, this is a potentially catchy, mid-tempo number and is available on Joey's *Demo's Old and New* CD.

Wish You Were Here

Personnel:
Pete Ham: vocals, guitar, keyboards
Tom Evans: vocals, bass
Joey Molland: vocals, guitar
Mike Gibbins: vocals, drums, keyboard
Horns by Average White Horns, arranged by Roger Ball; Orchestrations by Anne Odell
Recorded at Caribou Ranch, Colorado, USA and Air Studios, London, UK (April – July 1974)
Produced by Chris Thomas
Release date: October 1974
Highest chart places: UK: Did not chart, US: 148

As soon as the latest US tour had finished (April 1974), the band were instructed by their management to immediately commence the recording of their next album. With barely a day off to recover after the just-completed two-month touring jaunt around the US, the boys were whisked off to the Caribou Ranch recording studio based in Colorado. Exhausted, increasingly unhappy with management and lacking any new material, the band were understandably feeling incredibly upset and dejected at this situation. They would have much preferred a few months rest and relaxation and an opportunity to write some new songs, but, unfortunately, the demanding WB record deal (which stipulated that the group deliver two albums per year over a three-year period with a minimum of three singles per year as well) would not allow for this. Therefore, the band had no choice but to acquiesce and begrudgingly got down to the business of producing another new album. Chris Thomas was once again on board as producer and quickly perceived the sullen and discordant atmosphere. As he recalled in his 2019 interview with *CultureSonar*:

It just kept going down for them. It wasn't great during *Ass*, and by *Wish You Were Here*, they were completely down in the dumps. Nobody ever made a penny from Badfinger. Everything was fiddled away. I think Pete was upset that he never made any money from 'Without You'. They made no money ... None of them had anything, all fiddled away. It was a horrible situation to be in.

However, Chris did his best to gee the boys up at the beginning of the sessions as he later confirmed in the liner notes from *The Best Of Badfinger – Volume II* CD (Rhino Records, 1990):

Everyone was upset about management. We were all sitting around wondering, 'Do we really want to go ahead with it? Is there enough material?' Finally, I said, 'the only way around all the problems is we just have to make the best possible album.' And everyone agreed that was it!

81

Tom and Joey were particularly unhappy with management and the financial situation and, indeed, Tom even decided to quit at this point. However, due to management's refusal to buy him an airline ticket home, he ended up stuck and bored and reluctantly decided that he may as well play on the record.

However, despite this acrimonious backdrop, and with Chris Thomas' resolute encouragement, the band started to present a number of musical ideas and productivity was good. The final days of recording at Caribou Ranch took place during the first week of May. The band then returned to England and, after a short break, recommenced recording at the beginning of June at Air Studios in London. Productive sessions again ensured that by July, Badfinger had pretty much completed their new recordings. Chris Thomas then spent some time refining and mixing the album. This involved hiring an orchestral arranger to add some strings 'n' things to some of the songs, whilst the Average White Band's horn section was also recruited to augment a couple of the tracks. Apparently, the Velvet Underground's John Cale was the first choice for orchestral arranger, but when this fell through, Anne Odell was chosen instead.

By the end of July, the completed album had been mixed and was ready to go. The entire band was delighted with the final product and the general consensus within the camp was that this album was their best effort yet. Producer Chris Thomas later echoed this positivity in the online Bill Kopp-authored *Record Collector* article (November 2018): 'That was definitely the pinnacle of the records that I'd made up to that point. Even today, there's very, very little I would change on it.'

Regarding the LP cover, the group are shown as sailors partying in a Far Eastern bar evoking a sense of 'having a great time, wish you were here.'

However, before the record was even released, the curse of Badfinger struck again. During the late summer period of 1974, Pete Ham decided to quit the band. Fed up with what he perceived as a management takeover bid by Joey and, especially, Kathie Molland, Pete resolved to leave the band – from their point of view, the Mollands were incredibly dissatisfied with the existing management and their highly suspicious financial shenanigans. Joey explained the situation further to *Creative Loafing* in 2005:

> I had flown out to California and … while there, I met a lawyer who told me it was common knowledge in the industry that Badfinger was being screwed. It broke my heart. I flew to England to tell the band, but Peter didn't believe it.

With an imminent UK tour booked (due to start late September), a replacement for Pete was needed immediately and so it was that keyboardist Bob Jackson (ex-Indian Summer and ex-Ross) was hastily drafted in. As it turned out, Pete returned to the fold in a matter of a few weeks. There are conflicting reports as to why this sudden about-face, but according to the Ham camp, it was allegedly due to WB threatening to drop the group entirely if he left. Joey was not exactly happy to see the return of Pete, but, with Tom and Mike being more agreeable, Pete did indeed re-join and the band proceeded to complete a (month-long) half-hearted tour as a five-piece with Bob Jackson being retained. Once the tour was over (at the end of October), however, it was Joey's turn to say 'enough is enough' and he quit the band! Joey later discussed his decision to leave the band at this point (as detailed in the Dan Matovina biography):

I left the group because there was no way it could work. We talked and talked and talked about it. I wanted to get away from the managers and there was no way we could reach an agreement on it. It was obvious they weren't going to change the management. We were going to have the same people, the same organisation. It was going to be bullshit ... I couldn't do anything else. Pete was obsessed that my wife wanted to manage the band. Tommy was too. I know for a fact because they'd said things. They resented her.

Joey elucidated further on this entire situation in a more recent interview with *Guitar World* (in October 2020):

The problems really started when this guy, Stan Polley, got involved. Pete had a lot of faith in him, and I don't know why because the guy was a crook. That's what I call him – 'the crook.' It was just blatant. Pete and Tommy had been warned when the band left Apple and signed to Warners to get rid of him. Pete actually left the band at one time. He came back after a few weeks and wanted back in. I asked him what we were going to do about Stan, and he didn't want to do anything. I said, 'Well, what's the point in this?' We didn't have any money. Think about that: We were selling millions of records and were on the radio all day, all over the world. We were broke! We were driving second-hand cars. We got a salary of $300 a week. And then I quit – I just couldn't take what was going on anymore.

Amidst this period of turbulent chaos and turmoil, the album was finally released in November 1974. Despite no accompanying single and, again, very little promotion, early sales were modestly encouraging and the critical reaction was great. *Rolling Stone* were incredibly enthusiastic in their review of the new record:

Now, at last, they've made an album that derives a general style from what the band constructed on those [previous hit] singles: the captivating melodies, melancholy vocals and big bell-like rhythm guitars outlining a stirring, full-bodied sound ... *Wish You Were Here* is loaded with songs that are catchy and electric ... a wonderful album to play right through ... their most fully formed album.

Phonograph echoed these positive sentiments: 'All their patented strengths are displayed ... The album is bursting with hits ... there's not a weak track on the album ... a sparkling album, easily one of the year's best.' Meanwhile, *Cash Box*'s judgement on the new offering also revealed them to be ardent supporters of the new album:

> ...Badfinger continues its string of unique and challenging LPs with this dynamic collection of tunes guaranteed to bring a smile to your face and raise your spirits. Impeccable harmonies, crisp arrangements and excellent selection of material earmark this LP as a sure-fire winner.

Retrospective assessments have also been glowing in their endorsements. *Allmusic*, for example, had this to say about the album: '...a glistening, powerful rock record ... could have been a hit ... easily the most cohesive album the group ever recorded ... showcases each band member at a peak of songwriting.'

However, before the record had even had a chance to make a significant impact on the charts (at least in the US where the album had climbed to a promising 148 in the *Billboard* 200), a major disaster befell the band. Due to the misappropriation of the sizeable WB advance from an escrow account, WB instigated legal proceedings against the band and their management. WB also immediately ceased the distribution and promotion of the new album and, thus, after a mere seven-week existence, *Wish You Were Here* died a death. The band, who had felt so confident about the album, were completely devastated. Mike expressed his thoughts in the 1997 Gary Katz-directed *Badfinger* documentary:

> *Wish You Were Here* – it was [more] like, '*Wish You Were Where?*' They pulled it off the shelf. As soon as it was done ... I can't believe they did that, you know? They should have at least made some money off of it.

Joey also expressed his feelings in the *Badfinger* documentary:

> I know it was selling ... until [business manager Stan] Polley took the money from the escrow account. Unbelievable. He emptied a Warner Brothers escrow account, and Warners pulled the record from the stores immediately and sued Badfinger. We lost everything. Killed the record dead.

Producer Chris Thomas echoed the band's feelings in Dan Matovina's biography: 'We were all completely defeated when it got shelved ... I was incredibly disappointed.' However, as low as things were by the end of 1974, the following year would see the band fall even further as the most awful tragedy ultimately destroyed them – but I'll be discussing that in the next chapter.

For now, back to *Wish You Were Here*, and I would probably concur with the general critical consensus that this collection of songs presents us with their most consistent, finely wrought and beautifully realised piece of work.

This richly textured album is extremely well-crafted and contains many fine examples of classy, melodic and anthemic pop-rock. The record is emotionally engaging (most of the lyrics were written in response to the respective band members' woes at the time) and most of the band are performing at an absolute peak. Although the Beatles' influences are still there, thanks to some incisive production courtesy of Chris Thomas, a clearer band identity is ultimately revealed. The orchestral and horn arrangements also add a lovely splash of tonal lustre to proceedings. All in all, despite the incredibly trying circumstances surrounding the creation of this album, Badfinger managed to defy the odds and produce a truly exceptional piece of work.

The album was released on CD for the first time during the 1990s and subsequently reissued several times during the 2000s. The latest CD reissue came in 2018 with an 'Expanded Edition' release on the Real Gone Music label (with added bonus tracks – these bonus tracks mainly comprise new, alternate mixes created by Badfinger scholar Dan Matovina. They are not designed to be alternate 'final' mixes as such, but rather they present fans with an opportunity to gain further insight into the band's creative process and discover previously unused or buried musical parts).

'Just A Chance' (Ham)

The album bursts joyously into life with this rollicking and high-octane Pete Ham number which sets the tone for the rest of this brisk and vibrant record. Blazing electric guitars and pounding drums create a propulsive melody over which gorgeous, harmonised vocals glide effortlessly. This full-throttled, barnstorming opener was written by Pete in response to the hard time he was getting from certain factions within the Badfinger camp who were less than happy about his then-current love affair with Anne Ferguson, the estranged wife of one of the band's roadie's. Pete vented his frustrations in this song and his forceful vocals deliver the defiant lyrics with real bite:

> I won't tell you if it's short or long
> All I know is that it don't feel wrong
> You may say it's not a great romance
> But all we want from you is just a chance to try
> Any way we can
> Don't you think we know it hurts to hurt
> Won't you understand?

Joey performs a great, exuberant guitar solo mid-song and the injection of horns throughout the piece (courtesy of the Average White Band's horn section and credited as Average White Horns on the record) adds a lovely, rich texture to the instrumental background. This is simply a terrifically dynamic and stunning opening to the album that proffers the listener with a real statement of intent.

An 'alternate mix' of this song was released on the 2018 Expanded Edition CD reissue as a bonus track, whilst a solo demo version of the song is also available as a bonus track on the Japanese edition of Pete's 7 *Park Avenue* CD.

'Your So Fine' (Gibbins)

Written by Mike as a love song for his wife, this upbeat, country-tinged pop number was actually entitled 'You're So Fine', but due to a typographical error that was not spotted at the time (unbelievably!) it appeared erroneously as 'Your So Fine'. However, misspelling aside, this jaunty little tune maintains the high-energy established with the opening track and features Pete and Joey sharing harmonious lead vocals. The subtle use of harmonica adds to the country-pop recipe, as indeed does the charming fingerpicking throughout and the terrific slide guitar solo mid-song, both courtesy of Joey. The song climaxes with some lovely, jingle-jangle Byrds-esque guitar.

An 'alternate mix' of the song was also released on the 2018 Expanded Edition CD reissue as a bonus track.

'Got To Get Out Of Here' (Molland)

The first Joey-penned number to appear on the album, this rather moody tune finds Joey venting his frustrations of the time and clearly reflects the claustrophobic pressure that he was feeling with regards to management and career woes. The effective, world-weary vocals from Joey are carried along by a sparse and simple acoustic arrangement backed by a droning, church-like organ which imbues the tune with a suitably sombre ambience.

An 'alternate mix' of the song again appears on the 2018 Expanded Edition CD reissue as a bonus track.

'Know One Knows' (Ham)

Originally entitled 'No One Knows Me' and very autobiographical in nature, Pete later altered the lyrics to reflect his love for his new partner, Anne Ferguson and retitled it accordingly. The resulting tune is an absolutely joyous pop number, incredibly catchy and an obvious single choice. Bafflingly, however, it only appeared as a single in Japan (b/w 'Your So Fine', released January 1975) and was never released as a single anywhere else – quite what was going through WB's mind at the time is beyond me – this, again, could have provided the band (and the record label!) with a major chart hit. To my ears, this is nothing less than pure, unadulterated, power-pop perfection!

However, not everyone within the band was as enamoured with the song. Joey, reportedly, had his reservations about the track, feeling it was too pop for their then-current evolution. He was apparently sick of the pop thing at the time and wanted the band to be stronger and heavier. While I can certainly appreciate Joey's thoughts and concerns, I can only conclude that, ultimately, when guitar pop-rock is as gorgeously sublime and goosebump-inducing as this, it would have been a major crime had it not been included on the album – sorry, Joey!

Somewhat ironically, however, given his comments regarding the credibility of the song, it was Joey who suggested the idea which resulted in the most alluring part of the piece – Mika, the female Japanese singer with the Sadistic Mika Band (also produced by Chris Thomas), was recruited to seductively and sensually recite the chorus lyrics in Japanese over the mid-song guitar solo as per Joey's suggestion. Joey commented on this in the Michael Cimino-authored biography:

This was my idea, to have the Japanese girl speak in Japanese over the solo. I thought it was so romantic. The Japanese voice, and the words, and the way she said it. She's just saying the words 'Know one knows it, know one knows it' … It sounded good. I think it still sounds good.

An 'alternate mix' of the song was released on the 2018 Expanded Edition CD reissue as a bonus track, whilst a solo acoustic demo version is also available as a bonus track on the Japanese edition of Pete's *7 Park Avenue* album.

'Dennis' (Ham)

Another top-drawer tune from Pete, this one is dedicated to Anne Ferguson's son, Blair. Pete wasn't comfortable using Blair's actual name in the song and therefore used the metaphor of the mischievous comic strip character Dennis the Menace, which makes perfect sense given the lyrical references to a child teetering between mischief and innocence.

This track features a fairly progressive arrangement and can be viewed as comprising three distinct parts – first off, we have a couple of moderate, piano-backed verses crowned with heavy-ish *Abbey Road*-esque guitars and vocal harmonies. The song then abruptly changes gear and expresses a much lighter and more upbeat vibe via its unique chord structure, passionate lead vocals and exquisite backing vocal harmonies. The final section of the piece then sees an extended harmonious, choir-like coda with vocals chanting 'There's a way…' which is utterly beguiling. Producer Chris Thomas, however, later expressed some reservations about his creative input regarding the ending of the song (in his 2019 interview with *CultureSonar*):

I was thrilled with the album … My only regret is at the end of 'Dennis' … At the end, there are two minutes of overdubs and that was my idea. [But] It doesn't really add anything.

Personally, I think that, both compositionally and sonically, this song is amazingly strong and impressive.

An 'alternate mix' of this song was also released on the 2018 Expanded Edition CD reissue as a bonus track.

'In The Meantime' / 'Some Other Time' (Gibbins, Molland)

The first of two medleys on the album, the idea for combining these two unfinished songs into one piece of music came from producer Chris Thomas who, subsequently, freely admitted (in the online Bill Kopp-authored *Record Collector* article from November 2018): '...[it was] an idea I copied from The Beatles, from side two of *Abbey Road*.' Despite the obvious influence, the end result is absolutely inspired. A lush, symphonic fusion of progressive rock and pop-rock, this near seven-minute epic coupling of Gibbins and Molland musical ideas exudes a totally arresting quality with its ambitious, yet highly infectious, melody replete with beautifully elaborate orchestral backing and fierce guitar solos throughout.

The track begins with a rather eerie sounding forty-second sustained orchestral chord (courtesy of arranger Anne Odell's creative mind) before exploding into Mike's 'In The Meantime'. This section of the medley (a song about 'the decadent know-alls and bigheads' according to the song's composer in the Matovina tome) is a fantastic sounding piano-driven rocker that also features some amazing, riff-filled lead guitar from Pete Ham and majestic strings and horns. The arrangement is both intricate and unique and is probably the closest to prog rock that Badfinger ever got. The end result is dramatically compelling.

Mike performs the lead vocals admirably, too, although, reportedly, he apparently wasn't all that keen on doing them since he didn't really consider himself as a singer. Thankfully, producer Chris Thomas convinced him otherwise.

Just after the four-minute mark, 'In The Meantime' neatly segues into the second part of the medley, 'Some Other Time' (written by Joey). This piece again features stunning orchestral arrangements and great lead guitar parts working in unison to produce a fantastic, full-bodied sound. Joey's vocals also impress as he emotes about his respective relationships with management and other band members. Joey elaborated further on the song's message in the Michael Cimino-authored biography:

> The words were directly about my relationship with the band and my relationship with [business manager Stan] Polley, and what I thought about that. 'We've seen it before man/it's always the same. We know what you're doing/we think it's a shame. Gonna have to make a new start.' The words are directly about that. 'I can remember being in love with a friend of mine.' The friend is the band. 'I can remember knowing you better some other time.' It was direct. It was about that relationship.

This magnificent piece then climaxes with a very satisfying fusion of rock piano and guitar. It should be noted that, along with 'Know One Knows' and 'Should I Smoke', this medley got the bulk of orchestral arranger Anne Odell's input and it must be stressed that her orchestrations (as performed by the Martyn

Ford Orchestra) really enhance both parts of the medley and her creative input cannot be underestimated.

An 'alternate mix' of this medley was released on the 2018 Expanded Edition CD reissue as a bonus track.

'Love Time' (Molland)

Written as a love song for his wife, Kathie, this rather short and sweet Joey Molland-penned acoustic ballad is totally charming and features a short bridge with a perfect little guitar solo (courtesy of Pete). Being just over two minutes in length, this gorgeous little tune certainly doesn't outstay its welcome and subtly imbues the album with a nice hint of romance.

An 'alternate mix' of this song was also released on the 2018 Expanded Edition CD reissue as a bonus track.

'King Of The Load (T)' (Evans)

Tom Evans' only songwriting contribution to the album, this electric piano-laden tune, an ode to roadies, sadly lacks the same top-drawer quality of the other tracks on the album and, for me, is the weakest track on display and the (relative) low point of the album. It's not awful, by any means, but it just plods along unremarkably and it's ultimately all just a little forgettable and inconsequential.

According to Mike Gibbins, this song was thrown in at the last minute and laboriously done. To be brutally honest, all the hard studio work probably wasn't worth the effort as the end result is just so – average (sorry Tom)! On the plus side, the musicianship is faultless – great electric piano, strong lead guitar – but even the obligatory mid-song guitar solo fails to lift this track out of the doldrums!

As for the '(T)' in the song title, I'm still not entirely sure what it stands for! Extensive research has not revealed a definitive answer. It could possibly be in honour of a particular Badfinger roadie (one David 'Tag' Hall), but the absolute truth remains elusive!

'Meanwhile Back At The Ranch' / 'Should I Smoke' (Ham, Molland)

This album-closing medley (another Chris Thomas-inspired combination of unfinished song ideas) is another tremendous rocker that displays incredibly strong rhythms and melodies throughout. 'Meanwhile Back At The Ranch', the punchy, up-tempo opening section of the medley (penned by Pete Ham) features strong and extremely impassioned vocals from the song's composer:

If they only would let us know
Then we'd know just how far to go
But instead, they just tell us no, tell us no

The song canters along nicely, ably propelled by Mike's solid skin-pounding, until around the two-and-a-half-minute mark whereupon the piece seamlessly segues into the 'Should I Smoke' section. This emotionally charged part of the medley (written by Molland) carries much of the same drive as the first section, albeit accentuated by orchestration. Joey's vocals are top-notch and a sudden injection of horns at around the four-minute mark enhances the already stellar instrumental backing. The track comes to a glorious close with a magnificent, extended lead guitar solo from Pete – a perfect conclusion to the album.

This and the earlier *Abbey Road*-esque medley not only provide the cornerstones of the record but also show ample evidence of Badfinger convincingly moving away from standard pop-rock/rock 'n' roll into a newer, more progressive setting. Producer Chris Thomas later expressed his thoughts on the album's medleys in his 2019 interview with *CultureSonar*:

> I nicked an idea from Paul [McCartney], which he used on side 2 of *Abbey Road*. Stitching songs together to see if it fit. It helped with the songwriting … I just stitched two songs together to see if it would work. I can't quite remember, but it must have been one person had one song and another a different song. Let's see if they work. It's an extension of the verse-chorus thing. You can hear it on 'Without You', very clearly the difference between Pete's part and Tommy's. The Beatles used it on 'A Day In The Life', Paul's part is very different from the verses. It's part of the experiment to see if two very different pieces come together. That's all part of the process to see if it works and in this case, I think it did work.

An 'alternate mix' of this medley was released on the 2018 Expanded Edition CD reissue as a bonus track.

Other Contemporary Songs
'Queen Of Darkness' (Evans)
Originally written in 1972 and attempted in the studio during the *Wish You Were Here* recording sessions, this Tom Evans-penned number remained unreleased until 2018 when it was released as a bonus track on the Expanded Edition CD reissue of the album. It's a nice, up-tempo soft rocker with a buoyant, chugging rhythm and lyrics that display a satisfying bite. In my humble opinion, it would have served as a much better album offering from Tom than 'King Of The Load'. Yes, it needed a little bit more work in the studio to tighten it up a bit, but, ultimately, I believe this tune would have made a stronger addition to the record.

'It Doesn't Really Matter' (Ham)
This unreleased Ham-penned song from the period references Pete's relationship with Anne Ferguson (the estranged wife of Badfinger roadie, Ian 'Fergie' Ferguson) and the turmoil surrounding it – Pete's union with Anne was

not wholly welcomed within the Badfinger camp and this song dates from that period and, once again, finds Pete demonstrating his defiance:

> It doesn't really matter how they try
> They'll never break up you and I
> And though sometimes they'll make you cry
> There's nothing they can do
>
> It doesn't really matter how they sneer
> For you will always have me near
> From day to day, and year to year
> There's nothing they can do

This romantic ode to Anne is okay but veers a little too close to the twee side for my taste and although I appreciate the song's sentiment, I do find it a bit too sappy. A home demo version of this song is available on Pete Ham's 7 *Park Avenue* CD. An alternate acoustic guitar demo take was also made available on the bonus CD that accompanied the first edition of the Dan Matovina-authored band biography.

Head First

Personnel:
Pete Ham: vocals, guitar, synth
Tom Evans: vocals, bass
Bob Jackson: vocals, synth, piano, organ
Mike Gibbins: vocals, guitar, drums, percussion
Recorded at Apple Recording Studios, London, UK (1-15 December 1974)
Produced by Kenny Kerner and Richie Wise
Release date: November 2000
Note: Although this album was originally shelved (and didn't actually see the light of day until 25 years later when it was released by Snapper Music), I am inserting it here for analysis in its correct chronological position in terms of actual recording dates.

Once again, the band barely had a chance to catch its breath after the completion of the recent UK tour and the subsequent departure of Joey Molland from the ranks before they were instructed by management to initiate work on their next record. To make matters even worse, they were only going to be given two weeks to complete the recordings! This was all clearly being rushed through by their business manager (Stan Polley) in an attempt to obtain another cash advance from WB but, as detailed in the previous chapter, WB instead instigated legal proceedings against both the band and its management for a previously misappropriated cash advance. However, whilst these legal wranglings were developing in the background, the band found itself back in its old stomping ground of Apple Recording Studios where Badfinger were booked in to record their new album. Although the surroundings were familiar, there was a new production team at the helm this time around. Stan Polley brought over American producers Kenny Kerner and Richie Wise (who had just enjoyed success with the band Kiss) to weave their magic over the proceedings. Again, the band members were far from happy with this rush job situation but didn't feel like they had much choice at this point in time. In Dan Matovina's book, Mike recollected:

> We weren't getting paid regularly at this point and we thought, 'What are we doing this for, when we haven't even gotten the money for the last one yet?' Our hearts weren't in it. But being a musician, it was, 'At least we're doing something, at least we're playing music.'

So, the band spent the first two weeks of December (1974) feverishly writing and recording new material in a desperate attempt to get an album together and, rather admirably, by the end of this period, they had completed ten songs. Given the ridiculously quick turnaround time, the resultant album is pretty damn impressive too. Yes, it's very short (it only clocks in at just over the thirty-minute mark) and there are a couple of questionable inclusions on the record, but, I reiterate, the overall quality of what they achieved (effectively from scratch) in just a couple of weeks is amazingly good.

Many of the songs were, understandably, informed by the band's woes at the time so there is a real, delicious directness and bite to some of the lyrics. The musical performances are also terrific – Pete's guitar work is superlative throughout and he is ably supported by the solid musicianship of Tom and Mike on bass and drums, respectively. Bob Jackson, retained as a permanent band member after the recent tour and subsequent departure of Joey, also impresses greatly with his songwriting, vocal and keyboard skills. The loss of Joey obviously left a huge gap to be filled, in terms of songwriting and musicianship, and everyone stepped up to the plate magnificently. Bob Jackson, speaking to *The Strange Brew* in 2016, reflected on the *Head First* sessions:

It was gobsmacking for me, going into Apple in Savile Row. A tremendous buzz and sense of occasion. But this was tempered with the growing awareness that the business thing was not quite right. Our management instructed us to get the material written and complete everything ASAP to fulfil the Warner's contract. On top of all that, Joey Molland left the band. That's not the ideal way to start the creative process, but we just had to be efficient and get on with it. Considering all the circumstances, I feel we did OK…

After the recording sessions had concluded, rough mixes of the songs were quickly assembled and sent to WB for approval. Despite the burgeoning legal issues with WB, the band and management team obviously wanted to demonstrate that they were still working under contractual obligations. Sadly, however, WB rejected the rough mix of the album outright. Even without the ongoing legal issues between the two parties, I don't think WB were overly impressed with what they heard from the initial rough mixes. Another mix of the album was subsequently put together by Kenny Kerner and Richie Wise in early 1975, but this too was rejected.

This was all totally heart-breaking for the band and at this juncture, the entire band situation was becoming overwhelmingly distressing – *Wish You Were Here* had been withdrawn, *Head First* had been rejected, management and financial woes were prevalent (hardly any money was getting passed onto the boys in the band at this juncture). Pete, in particular, was feeling under tremendous strain at this point in time – he felt that his career was in tatters, he'd lost confidence in his songwriting abilities, he'd just bought a new house but was now in financial debt, he was expecting a new child with his partner, Anne Ferguson, and, slowly but surely, he'd come to realise that everyone's suspicions about Stan Polley and his financial shenanigans were indeed correct. Tragically, it all became too much for him, and a desperate and overwhelmed Pete Ham committed suicide by hanging himself in the garage of his new home. His death occurred on 24 April 1975, just three days before his 28th birthday.

He also left behind a suicide note in which he even cited Badfinger's business manager: 'P.S. Stan Polley is a soulless bastard. I will take him with me.'

This awful tragedy effectively ended the band (at least for the time being). *Head First* was never released at the time and, indeed, by the end of 1975, WB had terminated Badfinger's record contract and the band members went their separate ways. I'll pick up their respective tales in the following chapter.

As for *Head First*, fans finally got to hear the complete album (albeit in its original, rough mix form) when Snapper Music issued it as a 2-disc CD set in 2000 (the first disc contains the original rough mixes of the intended ten songs whilst the second disc contains demos recorded at around the same time). As asserted earlier, I believe this album is a great, solid little record which is tough yet melodic. It may be true that no individual songs shine quite as brightly as previous efforts, but as a cohesive whole, it really hangs together remarkably well. Realistically, it probably wouldn't have reversed their chart fortunes at that time even if it had been released, but it certainly wouldn't have shamed them either. I believe it stands as a robust and worthy addition to the Badfinger catalogue and, in an ideal world, they would have had more time in the studio to work on it. If they had, then maybe they could have developed and brought to fruition some of the more interesting ideas found on disc 2 of the Snapper release. Who knows, it may even then have scaled the same creative heights as *Wish You Were Here*. Stephen Thomas Erlewine's *AllMusic* review of the album offers a similar sentiment:

> *Head First* confirms that Badfinger had settled into a groove with *Wish You Were Here*, finding an effective middle ground between their pop gifts and hard rock inclinations, with both Ham and Tom Evans contributing equally strong works.

As for the cover of the Snapper release, the design has stayed true to the creative intent of Tom Evans. At the time, he envisaged the cover as being an image of a roaring lion's head, with the symbolisation being the band going 'head first' into the roaring lion's mouth. Bob Jackson later confirmed this in Dan Matovina's book: 'The idea came from Tommy. He wanted the LP cover to be a lion roaring. The idea was the situation we were in, how we were diving in, 'head first'.'

'Lay Me Down' (Ham)
This lead-off track, a mid-tempo pop-rocker penned by Pete Ham, was intended to be the album's accompanying promotional single. As you'd expect from Pete, it's a jaunty and catchy little ditty, but, in all honesty, it doesn't quite scale the heights achieved by Pete's previous power-pop classics. It does have the feeling of being a 'written to order' single, the lyrics, in particular, being ever so slightly trite and banal. This evaluation may seem overly harsh, but it's only because Pete had set such previously high standards with his songwriting.

However, despite the slightly formulaic feel to the song, it still ultimately delivers on its immediate intent to appeal melodically. Vocally, Pete still performs the song with complete conviction and he is ably supported by the band's usual blissful and harmonious backing vocals. Although the tune has a fairly standard guitar and keyboard-driven arrangement, the band's fully committed musicianship is top-notch and really helps sell the song. So, yes, this tune may be a little bit Badfinger by numbers, but the end result is still a rather satisfying and enjoyable slice of melodious guitar pop rock, which many lesser bands would love to have written.

A different mix of the song (Kerner and Wise's early-1975 remix version) can be heard on *The Best Of Badfinger, Vol. II* CD (Rhino Records, 1990).

'Hey, Mr. Manager' (Evans)
With Joey Molland having now exited the band, this left a huge gap to be filled in terms of the band's songwriting and Tom Evans well and truly stepped up to the plate on this record and grabbed the opportunity to re-establish himself as a major presence on a Badfinger album. Always one to need real emotional inspiration and stimulation in order to write songs, the band's management and financial woes at that time certainly provided the necessary impetus for Tom. For this album, he specifically wrote two songs pertaining to Badfinger's business manager, Stan Polley – this track and 'Rock 'N' Roll Contract'. On this particular track, Tom reveals just how aware he was that the band were being ripped off by Polley and he delivers the vicious and biting lyrical grievances with real gusto. Rather incongruously, the bitter lyrical content is all wrapped up in a wonderfully catchy and perky melody, with the keyboard foundation being punctuated by Pete's lovely lead guitar:

Waiting for the phone to tell me you and I are through
And I'm not alone, I guess that everybody wants it too
You got no feeling, you've been dealing all the wrongs
The lives you're stealing
Lord, I think you should be gone

Hey, Mr. Manager
You're messing up my life
Hey, Mr. Manager
Don't think I need that kind of strife

'Keep Believing' (Ham)
This sweet-sounding ballad, a lovely heartfelt ode to the recently departed Joey, is an impressively strong, melodic composition from Pete. Often one to write whilst wearing his heart on his sleeve, Pete offers up this subtle, tender and slightly sorrowful tune as a plea for Joey to keep faith in his career. Drums, bass and piano provide a solid foundation over which some delectable slide

guitar weaves in and out. Pete's voice is gorgeously earnest throughout and
his lead vocals are backed by some captivatingly lush vocal harmonies during
the choruses. The harmonious, choir-like voices at the climax of the song are
particularly stunning:

> I couldn't wish you any bad
> I only miss the many highs we had
> Our problems made it hard to smile
> But I still loved you all the while
>
> I can't deny that times have changed
> I only wish we could have rearranged it
> We were the pawns in someone else's game
> Keep believing, you can make it now

 A different mix of the song (Kerner and Wise's early-1975 remix version) can
again be heard on *The Best Of Badfinger, Vol. II* CD.

'Passed Fast' (Evans, Jackson)
This novel Tom and Bob co-write also sees the pair share lead vocal duties.
Moody and dramatic, this keyboard and guitar-driven piece opens with a
beautiful piano intro before Tom handles the first verse with his hoarse and
wavering vocals. Pete Ham's stirring and riveting lead guitar work propels
the song along before Bob takes his turn at the mic to deliver the second
verse in his best Steve Winwood-esque voice. The lyrics are powerful and
emotional and the heavier sound of the instrumental backing serves as a
perfect complement. Some further exquisite piano work ensues before the
song concludes with a near-minute long searing guitar solo courtesy of Pete.
This rather intense and introspective piece is a really good, solid album
track and showed that the Evans/Jackson songwriting combo had a lot of
potential.
   The Kerner and Wise early-1975 remix of the song can again be heard on *The
Best Of Badfinger, Vol. II* CD.

'Rock 'N' Roll Contract' (Evans)
Tom's second tune, directed specifically at the band's business manager,
Stan Polley, offers up another slab of bitter diatribe. Tom's lyrical tirade, once
again, pulls no punches in its explicit reference to the band's then-current
management problems:

> Wrapped up in a rock 'n' roll contract
> Lots of paper I had to sign lots of times
> Man told me not to worry 'bout the business
> Just keep on poppin' those hits...

...You made me your slave
Whatever God gave me
You took to the grave
Now it's gone

A heavy, dramatic opening featuring Mike's pounding drums backed with
Pete's lead guitar and the band's harmony vocals gives way to a perky, buoyant,
up-tempo rocker. Tom delivers an absolutely terrific rock vocal full of passion,
whilst the backing vocal choruses of 'Know you can' are equally impressive.
Another really solid album track with great musicianship from everyone
(emphatic lead guitar, pulsating bass line, energetic drum pattern, dramatic
piano chords), this rancorous ditty concludes with another sublime blast of
Pete soloing on lead guitar.

'Saville Row' (Ham)

This very brief (thirty-second) synthesiser instrumental snippet is a real oddity. Its
inclusion on the album seems utterly pointless and, in my humble opinion, adds
absolutely nothing to the record. Presumably titled in honour of the address of
their then-current recording studio, the title is actually misspelt on the Snapper
Music release and should, of course, read as 'Savile' rather than 'Saville' (although,
to be fair to Snapper, I have seen photographs of tracklisting documentation from
the time and it has been spelt both ways!). Regardless of spelling issues, this track
is utterly disposable and must only have been included due to the extremely rigid
recording time constraints at the time and paucity of useable recorded material.

Note: Original track listing documentation from December 1974 also
indicates that the intended duration of the piece was actually one minute. I'm
unsure as to why the Snapper Music version only runs to half that length.

'Moonshine' (Evans, Jackson, Gibbins)

A unique, three-way co-writing effort, this song boasts an appealingly gorgeous
and lilting country-esque melody. Featuring both Tom and Bob on lead vocals,
this soulful and heartfelt ballad is led by a strumming acoustic rhythm guitar
while an electric piano gently pushes the melody along. The bass and drums
maintain the beat perfectly whilst delightful lead guitar fills are supplied
courtesy of Pete. Tom and Bob both do sterling vocal work on their respective
verses and the full band backing harmonies are typically blissful. This tune
enjoys a very nice, laid-back and relaxing vibe and the beautiful melody gently
floats along, taking the listener with it.

Again, the Kerner and Wise early-1975 remix version can be heard on *The
Best Of Badfinger, Vol. II* CD.

'Back Again' (Gibbins)

Another country-flavoured ditty from Mike, this charmingly gentle and
unassuming acoustic-based ballad continues the relaxed and laid-back

ambience established in the previous track. It also provides another example of Mike's deceptively strong songwriting ability. Like many of Mike's Badfinger songs, it may, upon a first listen, seem a little understated and disposable (especially when instantly compared with the more commercial blasts of power-pop from his bandmates) but repeated listens reveal an incredibly strong and highly skilled songwriting talent. Mike's earnest vocal delivery is also effectively heartfelt and adds to the overall charm of the piece. The slightly incongruous injections of synthesiser throughout the track are also strangely appealing and add to the allure of the tune. Finally, there is some tasty harmonica work towards the end, which contributes to the country-tinged vibe and rounds off the track nicely.

'Turn Around' (Jackson)

Although he had only just been recruited into the band, Bob Jackson was strongly encouraged to present song ideas for consideration and, it has to be said, Bob really rose to the occasion. His previous co-writing efforts, detailed earlier, were great, but this number, written solely by Bob, allowed him to stand in the spotlight and present a song easily equal in quality to those proffered by his bandmates. Reflecting on the *Head First* period, Bob had this to say in a 2016 interview with *Band on the Wall*:

> Despite rising business pressures and Joey just quitting, the vibe between the four of us on the sessions was great. We got on well and supported each other and as a consequence, the song arrangements came together really quickly.

Boasting a complex and progressive arrangement, this is a fairly heavy, moody and bluesy tune, almost Clapton-esque in nature. Ominous sounding bass, drums and organ create a dramatic backdrop against which flourishes of Pete's rhythm and lead guitar appear, creating a terrific rock number. It's no surprise that Tom Evans was a massive fan of this 'gutsy' track. Vocally, Bob was pretty versatile, although, on this particular track, he again adopted his Steve Winwood-like voice and it suits the song perfectly (in general, Bob's vocals fitted in pretty well with the rest of the band and, if anything, provided the band's vocal sound with an appealingly, albeit slightly, rougher edge).

'Rockin' Machine' (Gibbins)

The album's closing track is a very short, country-esque oddity – a humorous, good-time tune, to be sure, but also a completely throwaway tune. Even the song's composer was bemused by its inclusion on the intended record, as Mike confirmed in Dan Matovina's biography: '[it was] something I wrote on the spot. That was just a joke. I couldn't believe it was used'. Pete's slide guitar and Bob's honky-tonk piano add to the country flavouring of the piece, but it still results in an utterly disposable one-and-a-half-minutes of record time.

Again, I can only assume that given more time to record the album, this track (along with 'Saville Row') would either have been developed more fully by the band or completely discarded in favour of one of the more interesting demo ideas they had knocking around at that time. Also, rather ironically, given the song's title, this is one of the least rocking songs on the record!

Demos & Bonus Tracks (Disc 2)
Most of these home demos are relatively short musical sketches and song ideas around the two-minute mark in duration (the entire running time of this second disc is less than half an hour!), but they do offer a tantalising glimpse at what could have been had there simply been more recording studio time available for the completion of *Head First*.

'Time Is Mine' (Ham)
This pretty, albeit very short, melodic snippet from Pete is a mainly instrumental home demo with some lyric-free vocal humming on top. It's an acoustic, country-tinged fragment but too short to be of any real consequence.

'Smokin' Gun' (Ham)
Again, this home demo displays just Pete and his acoustic guitar only. Dressed up in cowboy-esque lyrics, this tune could easily be seen as another dig at the band's business manager, Stan Polley. The song details the story of the 'smokin' gun'-wielding character Will Parker who, despite outwardly appearing as a good guy, is actually a bad guy who ends up shooting an innocent called Johnny, who just 'played the game.'

'Old Fashioned Notions' (Gibbins)
This piano demo from Mike boasts a really interesting and unique melody and showed real potential. It's such a shame that they didn't have the time to explore and develop this musical idea further. Once again, it reveals the burgeoning songwriting talent of Mike Gibbins at this time.

'Nothing To Show' (Ham)
Just Pete and his acoustic guitar again, this short, up-tempo demo again lyrically reflects his prevailing mood at the time:

Nothing to show for the hard work
Nothing to show for the time we've spent
Nothing to show for the hard times
Nothing to blow for the way we've spent

'You Ask Yourself Why' (Gibbins)

Featuring Mike on acoustic guitar, this melodic, Beatles-influenced demo again had great potential. Pete even supplies some nice slide guitar on this one too.

'Keep Your Country Tidy' (Ham)

A nice, acoustic, mid-tempo strum-along from Pete.

'To Say Goodbye' (Jackson)

This demo from Bob shows off his more gentle and melodic side. It's a sweet-sounding ballad featuring just him and his acoustic guitar. A very pretty and Beatles-ish tune.

'Queen Of Darkness' (Evans)

Different to the full-band studio outtake recorded during the *Wish You Were Here* album sessions (which was subsequently released in 2018 on the *Wish You Were Here* Expanded Edition CD, as detailed in the previous chapter), this demo version finds Tom backed only by an acoustic guitar and offers up a much bleaker version of the song in this stripped-back setting.

'I Can't Believe In' (Ham)

Another acoustic home demo from Pete and yet again, the song's lyrics seem to be directed at Stan Polley:

I can't believe in
Some of the stories
Some of the stories
They're saying 'bout you

I can't believe in
Some of the rumours
Quick growing tumours
They're making me blue

Sadly, the majority of these Ham-penned demos do seem to confirm that Pete's issues with Stan Polley (and, indeed, the music industry as a whole) were becoming dangerously and worryingly all-consuming at this point in time.

'Thanks To You All' (Gibbins)

Revealing that old Beatles influence again, this melodic, acoustic-based Mike demo is another idea that had great potential if only there had been more time to develop it further.

'Lay Me Down' (Ham)
This home demo version of the album track features just Pete and his acoustic guitar and reveals the creative birth of the song. What's interesting to note is that the melody is already pretty much fully-formed and it seems as though the tune was simply fleshed out in the studio with the backing of the full band.

Other Contemporary Songs
'Helping Hand' (Ham)
This home demo, one of the last songs ever written by Pete, is a real cry for help, with the lyrics revealing a desperately troubled Pete reaching out to his partner at the time (Anne Ferguson), seeking her strength, guidance and support. Pete's complex emotional make-up was almost always best articulated via his songs and this is a perfect example of that. Not for the first time, though, Pete manages to lighten the overall mood and feel of the song by encasing his emotional plea in a fairly upbeat and poppy melody:

> All I need is my lover
> Someone who'll make me feel okay
> Any time of the day
> But we need to discover
> Some way to soothe our blues away
> On the darkest of days
>
> And when I need a helping hand
> Oh, my love, I wish you'd understand
> Wish you'd feel inside my mind
> And join in with the things that you find

This home demo is available on Pete's *Golders Green* CD.

'Just How Lucky We Are' (Ham)
Another maudlin demo recorded by Pete circa 1975, this one again references his relationship with Anne Ferguson. Pete's vocal performance is heartfelt and sincere and delivered over a simple but pleasant-sounding melody. The home demo is available on Pete's 7 *Park Avenue* album. An alternate acoustic guitar demo, including extra verses not on the 7 *Park Avenue* version, was also made available on the bonus CD given away with the first edition of the Matovina-authored band biography.

'Ringside' (Ham)
An incredibly melancholic home demo from the period detailing Pete's feelings of bitterness towards a music industry seemingly oblivious to his suffering:

Take your seat by the ringside
Watch them bidding for your blood
Who will own you tomorrow?
Will you be misunderstood?
Take me back to the father
Take me, take me, take me home
For I can't bear to feel the sorrow
Of the evil that you've shown...

This home demo is also available on Pete's 7 *Park Avenue* CD. Different, alternative versions of this song were also made available on both of the respective bonus CDs given away with the first and second editions of the Matovina book. Interestingly, the version found on the second edition's bonus CD is the first actual demo version with only one verse and chorus completed at this point.

'No More' (Ham)

This home demo, featuring Pete on electric guitar, is probably the starkest of all the demos written and recorded by Pete during this period. This song effectively serves as a suicide note and is devastatingly sad and heart-breaking to listen to. However, Pete again somehow still manages to wrap up all of this personal angst in a beautiful, sweet-sounding melody which almost succeeds in diverting attention away from the incredibly dark and depressing lyrical content:

Drunken days, drunken nights
Someone please turn out the light
I can't face the mirror anymore
Move along, magic gone
Someone else can sing my song
I can't lift my head up off the floor
No, no, no, no more

One version of this home demo can be found on Pete's 7 *Park Avenue* CD. A different version (with slightly amended lyrics and a modified title, 'No, Don't Let It Go') was released on an extremely limited-edition vinyl single (500 copies) issued in 2013 on the Without You Music label (b/w 'You're Such A Good Woman', a 1972 home demo – detailed in an earlier chapter). In this alternate version, the lyrics are aimed at another person rather than being written in the first person.

Airwaves

Personnel:
Tom Evans: vocals, bass
Joey Molland: vocals, guitars, electric piano
Joe Tansin: vocals, guitars
Ken Harck: drums
Andy Newmark: drums
Steve Foreman: percussion
Nicky Hopkins: piano, organ
Duane Hitchings: piano, synthesiser
Peter Clarke: legs, hands and feet
Recorded at Stickley Manor (aka the Annex), San Fernando Valley, Los Angeles,
California (October – December 1978)
Produced by David Malloy
String arrangements by David Campbell
UK release date: May 1979
US release date: March 1979
Highest chart places: UK: Did not chart, US: 125

After the tragic death of Pete Ham and the subsequent dropping of Badfinger from WB, the remaining band members, unsurprisingly, had little interest in carrying on Badfinger at that time and they all drifted off into other various musical ventures. Joey Molland formed the band Natural Gas with, amongst others, Jerry Shirley (ex-Humble Pie). They released an album in 1976 and toured briefly (supporting Jerry's old Humble Pie buddy, Peter Frampton, on his global conquering *Frampton Comes Alive* tour) before folding after finding little commercial success. In late 1975, Tom Evans reunited with Bob Jackson and together with a couple of other musicians, formed The Dodgers. They managed to release a few singles during 1976, but they too met with little commercial success. However, after starting work on an album in 1977, Tom was kicked out of the band (allegedly because of problems associated with his not insignificant consumption of alcohol).

Sometime during 1977, Joey Molland was approached by a couple of US-based musicians, drummer Kenny Harck and guitarist Joe Tansin, with a view to forming a band. He liked some of their musical ideas and started jamming with them. Things went well, but they soon realised that they needed a bass player, so who better to ask than Joey's old bandmate, Tom Evans. After listening to some of their new stuff, Tom was suitably impressed and agreed to join the new band in early 1978. Some full-band demos were promptly recorded and shopped around various record labels and it wasn't long before the demos attracted the interest of Elektra/Asylum Records. At this point, the new band still needed a name. According to Joey (in Michael Cimino's biography), it was actually Elektra who encouraged them to use the old Badfinger moniker:

[Steve Wax, President of Elektra/Asylum Records] said, 'Call it Badfinger. It sounds like Badfinger. Listen to it. With you guys singing, it sounds like Badfinger, so call it Badfinger.' Tommy and I were kind of a bit iffy about it, but we went along with it.

This decision to use the old band's moniker was, and indeed still is, a particular sticking point for a lot of fans and a bugbear for many. There are many fans out there who don't consider this to be a bona fide Badfinger project due to the fact that it's only Tom and Joey involved. I, personally, do not adhere to this school of thought and feel that, although missing Pete and Mike's voices, it still stands as a valid line-up. To be fair, using the old name was realistically a sensible thing to do too, given the doors it would inevitably open for them and the subsequent marketing power it would give them.

Anyway, with the band's name decided upon, a record deal with Elektra was duly signed and the band set about creating their comeback album. A number of potential producers were considered, but the final choice was David Malloy, who had then just recently enjoyed big success in the country music field. The band took up residence at the Annex in the San Fernando Valley and were awarded a fairly modest budget by Elektra to complete the album. Things started off fairly well, but it wasn't long before band relationships began to deteriorate against a backdrop of drink, drugs and interpersonal jealousies. Drummer Ken Harck apparently became obsessed with perfecting his drum sound and began telling the engineer and producer how to do their jobs. This obviously didn't go down too well with people and so Harck was duly sacked! At this point, Mike Gibbins' name came up as a replacement. Mike, who had kept himself busy since 1975 playing drums for various bands and artists (including Bonnie Tyler), was interested in joining and flew over to California. However, he only managed to last a few sessions before falling out with producer Malloy. Malloy deemed Mike's drumming as unsatisfactory and booted him off the project. Reliable session drummer Andy Newmark was then brought in to complete the recording sessions.

The final record comprised nine tracks (although with the introductory track only being about 30 seconds in length, it was really only eight tracks) and the general feeling within the band camp regarding the end result was mixed. Certainly, the overall consensus was that the record had ended up with a different sound than that first envisaged when the original demos had been cut. Indeed, a lot of Badfinger fans (then and now) agree that David Malloy lacked the necessary feel for pop-rock production and essentially sucked the raw rock out of the band. Joe Tansin appeared to support this sentiment that they chose the wrong producer when his feelings on the matter appeared in Dan Matovina's biography:

David Malloy was a mismatch, period. He was a country producer. There was no connection to us at all. The original concept was to sound like the band used to. That's what we did with the demos and everybody loved them. It hadn't needed to change a lot.

Unhappy with how the entire project had turned out, Tansin decided to quit the band whilst the record was still being mixed. Reflecting back on the project in the liner notes to the 1999 CD reissue of the album, Joe Tansin concluded that: 'To me, the making of this album has some bittersweet memories. But despite some bad business decisions and personal differences, some great music still managed to emerge.' Joey Molland, on the other hand, has always felt more positivity towards the album and, in Michael Cimino's biography stated:

I think *Airwaves* sounds really good. I think it stands up even today as a good sounding record. I don't think it was right for the times, the sound of it ... I think Badfinger and contemporary sound parted ways right there ... Things were changing ... I thought we went in a traditional direction with David Malloy. I think it's a good record, I'm not denying it, but I don't think the sound of it was right for the times and I think that's why it wasn't a hit.

Reflecting on the failure of the *Airwaves* record in more recent years, Joey reiterated his thoughts in a 2014 interview with *Something Else!*:

I've thought about this. The music was changing at that point; the sound of music was changing. There were bands like Toto and the Cars where the production values were so different than what we had been used to. I think with that record, it just fell right through the cracks. It was because of the changes in musical styles. Badfinger, all of a sudden, sounded a little bit old fashioned. We tried our best, but music changed – as it always does. It's one of those things. Timing again, I guess.

Producer David Malloy also has fond memories of working with Badfinger and commented in Dan Matovina's tome that:

I got a lot out of working with them ... I thought some of the criticism for the album was a bit harsh. There were some nice cuts. 'Lost Inside Your Love' is a beautiful song. I was proud of that. 'Sail Away' was real pretty. But overall, the record was against the flow of the times.

The LP was issued in the US in March 1979 with a front cover featuring side profile headshots of Joey and Tom superimposed on a green radar screen. Critical expectation had been fairly high but, upon release, the actual critical reception was a little underwhelming: *Rolling Stone* was unconvinced by the new offering:

...with the exception of 'Love Is Gonna Come At Last' and 'The Winner', two effervescent entries propelled by a choppy, John Lennon-like guitar,

Airwaves suffers from a bad case of weak knees. Badfinger, when faced with the dilemma of pop versus pap, opts for an uneasy commercial compromise that renders even a forceful rocker like 'Sympathy' impotent with a flaccid disco beat. Similarly, such dramatic ballads as 'The Dreamer' and 'Sail Away', for all their atmospheric high harmonies, are hurt by David Campbell's wimpy string arrangements and the dryly unimaginative production of David Malloy, an Eddie Rabbitt/Stella Parton veteran with no apparent feel for Anglo-American pop.

Stereo Review, meanwhile, made the following observations:

Two of the original members of Badfinger ... are here backed by studio musicians on what is less a comeback album than an attempt to capitalise on whatever value is left in the Badfinger name. The original Badfinger had such an arresting sound that for a time it was thought they might possibly be the new Beatles, not imitators or successors ... *Airwaves* has some good material – Molland's 'Love Is Gonna Come At Last' and Joe Tansin's 'Sympathy' – and some good performances, but I think the name 'Badfinger' ought to be permanently retired. While this is not entirely a case of false advertising, it is hardly in the best of taste.

Trouser Press was similarly guarded in its assessment of the new record:

Guitarist Joey Molland and bassist Tom Evans have made *Airwaves* the insidiously pleasant pop album one might have predicted a Pete Ham-less Badfinger would make: high on melody, direct in lyric but somewhat diffuse in focus ... *Airwaves* remains a classy encapsulation of Badfinger trademarks: quasi-McCartney vocals, thick guitars and elegant melodies ... In the end, good as some of it is, *Airwaves* doesn't quite hold together as an LP...

Elsewhere, there was more explicit negativity. The *NME* described the album as having 'a rather vapid tunefulness' whilst *Creem* complained that 'it just isn't the Badfinger that I came to know and love somewhere a long time ago.' As for retrospective reviews of the album, similar sentiments have consistently been expressed. *The All-Music Guide to Rock* (in 1995), for example, echoed the thoughts of those original, contemporary album reviews:

Using the magic of overdubbing and a complement of star studio musicians, Tom Evans and Joey Molland take a respectable shot at recreating the three-part harmonies and pop sheen of the early '70s ... Often, however, the material is only pedestrian, and although this album actually did a little better commercially than the group's two Warner Bros. albums of 1974, it didn't make for a real comeback.

Two promotional singles were lifted from the record, 'Lost Inside Your Love' and 'Love Is Gonna Come At Last', but neither really helped improve sales of the album (although the latter did actually chart, peaking at #69 on the *Billboard* chart). In addition to some promotional TV appearances, a supporting US tour was also put together with two new band members quickly enlisted to join Joey and Tom – drummer Peter Clarke ('Clarkie' – who had actually performed on the *Airwaves* title track, albeit just in terms of supplying a 'legs, hands and feet' beat!) and ex-Yes keyboardist, Tony Kaye. The tour went down well but album sales remained stagnant and the *Airwaves* record eventually peaked at #125 on the *Billboard* 200. Disappointed with the sales performance of the record, Elektra decided not to go ahead with a second album and promptly dropped Badfinger from its roster.

Personally, I do like the album. It's definitely too short and could do with a couple of additional tracks to bolster the record but what we do get is compositionally and sonically pretty strong. The trademark harmonies are still there and the Beatles-esque influence remains intact. Yes, by the very nature of Pete and Mike's absence from the record, it is Badfinger-lite, but I still believe the end result proffers us with a good, solid, entertaining and melodic album.

The album first appeared on CD in 1999 on the Permanent Press record label (with added bonus tracks) and was reissued again in 2004 on Wounded Birds Records (this time, with no bonus tracks).

'Airwaves' (Molland, Evans)

The album starts with this brief, 30-second, acoustic-based intro. The actual riff was taken from a song Joey had been working on called 'My Old Lady' about his wife, Kathie. In this opening number, Joey fingerpicks the funky lick while Tom Evans scats over the top. As mentioned earlier, their old drummer mate, Peter Clarke (aka 'Clarkie'), who later joined them for the *Airwaves* tour, contributes some 'legs, hands and feet' to the tune, which basically entailed Clarkie walking around the studio clapping his hands to the beat! This fleeting musical ditty barely gets a chance to breathe before it abruptly segues into track number two.

'Look Out California' (Evans)

After the slightly false start of the title track, the album kicks off properly with this extremely lively and energetic rocker. This spirited little number boasts an appealingly catchy chorus hook and a great vocal performance from Tom. His enthusiastic yelling of 'Back on the airwaves!' reveals a man who is clearly very happy to be back in the limelight. The very literal lyrics essentially detail Tom's excitement at being back in the band and his passionate vocal delivery is totally compelling. According to Tom, as stated in the Elektra/Asylum Records press release at the time:

'Look Out California' is just a song I wrote when I knew I was really coming over here [to America]. It was cold and raining in England at the time.

California seemed like such a good idea at the time, so much to look forward
to, you know? That's exactly what I feel ... look out, I'm coming!

The track mellows out a little mid-song with the introduction of a synthesiser
(courtesy of Duane Hitchings) to back Tom before the tune blasts off again
with the aid of a scintillating lead guitar solo from Joey. This track is also one
of two on the record that features drummer Kenny Harck on drums before he
was sacked. All in all, this good-time rock 'n' roll tune delivers a very enjoyable
listening experience.

'Lost Inside Your Love' (Evans)
Released as a single A-side (b/w 'Come Down Hard'): March 1979 (US), did not
chart; May 1979 (UK), did not chart
This track, released as a single in both the US and UK, is a gem of a song
and is probably the closest thing we get to that old classic Badfinger sound
on this record. Featuring a really strong and pretty melody and an awesome
Beatles-esque bridge, this vivacious power-pop ballad is terrific and really
should have made some sort of impact on the charts. With its gorgeously
captivating refrain, lush backing harmonies and sterling musicianship
throughout (including Nicky Hopkins on acoustic piano), this is definitely
one of Tom's best ballads. His vocals are, once again, spot on and Joey also
gets to show off his admirable lead guitar skills. A promotional video for the
song was also shot, but it, unfortunately, failed to help elevate sales of the
single and, rather perplexingly, it completely flopped on both sides of the
Atlantic.

Tom's piano demo from 1977 was made available on the bonus CD that
accompanied the first edition of the Matovina-authored band biography.

'Love Is Gonna Come At Last' (Molland)
Released as a single A-side (b/w 'Sail Away'): March 1979 (US), chart #69; July 1979
(UK), did not chart
A catchy and breezy power-pop tune, this Joey-penned track serves up a very
fine and pleasant-sounding listening experience even if it doesn't quite scale
the same creative heights as 'No Matter What' and 'Day after Day'. Featuring a
fairly moderate strumming beat punctuated by attractive slide guitar fills, the
lilting and engaging melody carries Joey's nicely sung lyrics along in a very
appealing way. The resultant sound is infectiously upbeat and the uplifting
and feel-good nature of the song makes for an exceedingly charming tune.
According to Joey, as stated in the Elektra/Asylum Records press release at the
time:

It's a song about hope – that's the real thing I get from it. It's something
we believe. I think this one sounds most like the things we did in the past,
brought up to date.

Again, a promotional video featuring a band performance of the track was shot to help boost sales of the single, this time resulting in the song enjoying a brief residency in the *Billboard* charts (peaking at #69 during April 1979).

'Sympathy' (Tansin)

This track was penned by new guitarist Joe Tansin and is actually a pretty decent song. However, this number, more than any other on the album, often suffers a bit of a critical bashing, mainly due to the disco beat applied to it during production. I think, compositionally, it's fundamentally fairly strong, but I would probably tend to agree that, in all honesty, the track does indeed suffer from the production choices made and results in a slightly flaccid tune. In defence of the production applied to this particular song, David Malloy (in Dan Matovina's book) has explained his decision-making at that time:

> The thing was, we were making that album at the absolute height of disco. We were making a Badfinger record and the record company promotion people were going, 'Huh?' It was because of the pressure I felt from the record company, and the band not having itself together, that we went for that. Granted, the kick drum is ridiculous. For Tommy, disco was the last thing he wanted to know about. But both Tommy and Joey were a little reserved in their opinions around me. They didn't challenge me a lot.

However, disregarding the disco vibe for a moment, there are still many positives to be found – Tom's lead vocals are reliably sound and his harmonies with Joey are great; the song's composer impresses on lead guitar and there is also some very nice electric piano courtesy of Joey. This is also the second track that features drummer Kenny Harck before he was replaced by session drummer Andy Newmark.

'The Winner' (Tansin)

Joe Tansin's second composition on the album, this is another solid and well-written tune. Featuring a confident-sounding Joey on lead vocals, this effervescent little number is propelled along by some nice choppy guitar. Instrumentally, Joe's lead guitar is enhanced throughout by both strings and synthesiser fills (again, courtesy of Duane Hitchings). The vocal harmonies impress, as expected, and overall, this is a very likeable and upbeat rocker, contemporary yet still distinctly Badfinger sounding.

'The Dreamer' (Molland)

A great Molland-penned bluesy power ballad, this tune features another strong and confident vocal performance from the song's writer. The melody is strong and appealing and the musicianship throughout is once again of the highest calibre – great lead guitar work from Joe Tansin (especially his terrific bluesy solo), lovely piano and Hammond organ sounds courtesy of Nicky

Hopkins, atmospheric high harmonies from Tom and Joey and all topped off by an extremely attractive orchestral backdrop. This slower tempo number ultimately stands as a really strong and well-written composition (indeed, when interviewed in 2013 by *RAWkin' Rik*, and asked about what his favourite Badfinger tune was that he had played on, Joe Tansin replied: 'Probably 'The Dreamer', still love the guitar solo.').

In the Elektra/Asylum Records press release at the time, Joey had this to say about the song:

> It's like a story song. Sometimes it seems to me to be about the music business and sometimes about life. I dream all the time, and this seems to be one of my dreams about the history of the rock musician. It began as a song about somebody who was fighting himself, and finally decided he could win.

'Come Down Hard' (Molland)

This Joey Molland rocker is all about a love affair breaking down (the girl in the relationship has all these plans laid out but, due to some two-timing, things don't pan out quite as she had hoped, so she 'comes down hard' as she faces up to the failed romantic liaison) and gets off to a dynamic start courtesy of Andy Newmark's pounding drums and Joe Tansin's lead guitar. Joey rocks out in a suitably confident manner on lead vocals and the song is driven along at a fair old pace by the combined force of guitars and drums. This is yet another solid and perfectly serviceable rocker that happily sustains its listening pleasure for the near four-minute runtime.

'Sail Away' (Evans)

This incredibly beautiful Tom Evans-penned piano ballad closes the album in a charmingly graceful manner. Featuring some heavenly piano work from Nicky Hopkins backed by David Campbell's impeccably arranged strings, this very pretty and sweet-sounding tune boasts an undeniably McCartney-esque melody. Tom once again impresses vocally and he emotes in a delightfully romantic fashion. This winsome and rather fetching little ditty provides a lovely and satisfying end to the album. This is what the song's composer had to say about the track in the Elektra/Asylum Records press release at the time: 'I think it's pretty, really pretty. The basic idea is when you feel fed up, what will you do? I think all of us just … sail away!'

Other Contemporary Songs
'One More Time' (Tansin)

This unreleased studio outtake from the *Airwaves* sessions finally saw the light of day on the 1999 CD reissue of the album (Permanent Press Recordings). Quite why it wasn't released at the time is a bit of a mystery since the (barely half an hour in duration) album not only needed more material on it anyway, but this is also a pretty fine track in its own right. Joe Tansin, the song's composer, actually sings lead on this one and his vocals are perfectly decent. It's an acoustic-based, slower tempo ballad which doesn't sound a million miles away from something ex-drummer Mike Gibbins might have penned. Tom Evans provides the pleasing harmony vocals and the distinctive cardboard box backbeat comes courtesy of Kenny Harck. There's also some nice lead guitar from Joey throughout and, overall, it's a real shame that this sweet-sounding contribution from Joe wasn't included on the final album.

Note: On the 1999 Permanent Press CD reissue, there are also four other bonus tracks – three of which were apparently written at the time of the *Airwaves* sessions but not recorded until a lot later on by either Joe or Joey, respectively. The final bonus track was a brand-new, unreleased studio track recorded by Joe Tansin. I, therefore, won't be discussing these tracks.

'Come And Get It' (Remake) (McCartney)
Recorded at Sound City (Van Nuys, Los Angeles, California) for the K-Tel record label (known for its reissuing of old hits, which were often re-recorded versions which allowed for easier rights clearance), this remake of their old McCartney-penned hit was produced simply for the money! The track was recorded after the *Airwaves* promotional duties had concluded and featured the following line-up – Tom Evans, Joey Molland, Tony Kaye and Peter Clarke. This track ended up on the following album releases: *The Legendary Sixties* (Arcade Records, 1983) and *Hit Reunion* (Era Records, 1983).

Say No More

Personnel:
Joey Molland: vocals, guitars
Tom Evans: vocals, bass
Tony Kaye: keyboards
Richard Bryans: drums
Glenn Sherba: guitar
Recorded at International Sound, Miami, Florida (September – November 1980)
Produced by Jack Richardson and Steve Wittmack
US release date: January 1981
Highest chart place: US: 155

Using some of the money earned from the K-Tel commissioned remake of 'Come And Get It' (see the previous chapter for details), the band set about cutting some new demos with a view to attracting a new record contract since Elektra had abruptly dropped them after the commercially disappointing *Airwaves*. A three-song demo tape was subsequently sent out to various record labels, but interest in signing the band was not particularly high, with Badfinger pretty much viewed by the industry as a well and truly spent force. In fact, it took several months to garner a label's interest and it wasn't until the second half of 1980 that the newly formed, Florida-based Radio Records (affiliated with Atlantic Records) offered them a deal.

Recording sessions for the new record were scheduled for a September start with Jack Richardson (best known for his work with The Guess Who and Alice Cooper) at the production helm (interestingly, Steve Wittmack is also credited as co-producer on the record but, according to Joey Molland in Michael Cimino's biography, he was actually just the record company's top A&R man). Joining Joey, Tom and Tony this time around were drummer Richard Bryans and guitarist Glenn Sherba. Initially, Tom's songwriting pal, veteran musician Rod Roach, also attended the sessions but didn't end up staying around too long (by all accounts, Joey and Rod didn't exactly hit it off). The band didn't waste any time recording the new record and the sessions were completed by November.

Despite the usual creative arguments and backdrop of record company/ management business issues, the resulting ten-track album is actually a pretty solid effort. It serves up a fairly well-produced and back-to-basics, good-time rock 'n' roll sound which still retains the usual Badfinger tropes (emotional ballads, catchy pop and hook-laden rock 'n' roll). The LP, featuring cover art by Peter Max (renowned for his psychedelic and pop artwork in the late 1960s), was released in January 1981 (in the US and Canada only – there was no UK release) to little fanfare. Three singles in total were lifted from the record, but only the first of these managed to bother the charts. 'Hold On' peaked at #56 on the *Billboard* chart and on the back of this minor hit, the record company wanted the band to go out and tour. However, the band decided to hold off on touring the album until the LP had gained some momentum (hoping that a hit record would get them a headline tour rather than a small club tour). This proved to be a poor decision as the record company soon got fed up and disillusioned with the band's decision and promptly pulled the plug on any further significant promotional support.

So, with no supporting tour and just a couple of promotional TV appearances, the new record ultimately only reached a lowly #155 on the *Billboard* 200 and quickly sank without trace. Reviews at the time were inevitably scarce, but at least they were generally positive in nature. *Trouser Press* declared that Badfinger were '...back on the right track...' whilst *Seventeen* stated that the LP contained '...a rollicking group of tunes guaranteed to have you dancing your feet off.' *Allmusic*'s retrospective assessment was a little more scathing:

> ...they sound more like a band on this record than they did on its predecessor ... but that is not an improvement ... a shadow of former glories ... it only confirmed that Badfinger was no longer a record seller.

The general fan consensus seems to be that although *Say No More* perhaps lacks the standout tracks that *Airwaves* has, this record proffers a better-produced sound and an overall stronger and more consistent listening experience. I think I would concur with that opinion. However, upon my first listen to the record, I remember feeling pretty disappointed with it initially – to my ears, it seemed that any resemblance to the Badfinger of old had completely disappeared. It was only upon repeated return visits to the album that the core Badfinger styles became more evident to me and the strength and quality of the music contained within revealed itself. As mentioned above, the emotional ballads and catchy, melodic pop-rockers are still present and correct, they're just wrapped up in a more organic, back-to-basics cloak of rock 'n' roll sound. The trademark harmonies can even be heard, too, albeit in a much more subtle and muted fashion.

Compared to the preceding *Airwaves*, the boys certainly tend to rock out more on this record and the resulting tunes, benefitting from the rawer production, offer listeners a rockier, rather than poppier, sound – but it is still, undoubtedly, the sound of Badfinger. Indeed, the resultant sound of the record was completely in line with the band's initial ambitions. In an October 1981 interview with *Goldmine* magazine, Joey had this to say about the new record:

> We wanted to do an album that sounded like the group, like when we go on stage and play. We didn't want to find ourselves in the position that we were in before. We did this album with that in mind, and we got a couple of young guys, the drummer, Richard Bryans, a fabulous guitar player, Glenn Sherba and of course, Tony Kaye.

However, having said this, this is also the reason why the record probably failed (and why the album wasn't even released in the UK). In a musical environment that was, at that time, enthusiastically embracing the more modern sounds of 'new wave/post-punk/synth-pop', what chance of success did this retro-sounding rock 'n' roll record really have, no matter how good it was? Sadly, *Say No More* proved to be the band's swan song as the looming dark clouds of depression and further tragedy gathered on the horizon.

This album was first issued on CD in 2000 (on the Real Music label) and reissued again in 2015 (this time, on the UK-based Gonzo Multimedia label). There were no additional bonus tracks on either release.

'I Got You' (Molland)
Released as a single A-side (b/w 'Rock N' Roll Contract'): April 1981 (US), did not chart
The album sets out its stall with this opening salvo of old school, good-time rock 'n' roll. Composed by Molland, this rousing tune kicks off with a blast of rockabilly guitar quickly followed by some thunderous drum pounding and impressive Jerry Lee Lewis-style piano work before Joey's vocals take flight. It's an engagingly buoyant and effervescent little number that bristles with energy throughout and launches the album in a suitably irresistible manner. Released as the second single from the album, this snappy dose of boogie rock, unfortunately, failed to dent the charts but still remains an impressive start to the record.

'Come On' (Evans)
This energetic Tom Evans-penned rocker exudes a McCartney/Wings vibe wherein sizzling guitar licks combine with exuberant rock 'n' roll piano chords to produce a dynamically driven piece. Tom delivers some great enthusiastic vocals that are enhanced by Beatles-esque harmonies that filter through in the song's refrain. The lively tempo and high energy established in track one are maintained with this rollicking follow-up.

'Hold On' (Evans, Tansin)
Released as a single A-side (b/w 'Passin' Time'): February 1981 (US), chart #56
Exhibiting a slightly slower tempo than the first two songs on the record, this nice, catchy pop-rocker nonetheless still finds itself driven along by some similarly solid rock 'n' roll drumming and choppy piano sounds. Chosen as the lead single from the album, this Tom Evans and Joe Tansin co-write was actually a leftover from the *Airwaves* period (Joe was apparently responsible for the chorus but was not actually credited on the original LP for some reason – however, his omission from the songwriting credits was subsequently rectified with later CD reissues).

The track, again betraying an obvious McCartney/Lennon influence in its composition and arrangement, features an appealing lead vocal from Tom that is also redolent of McCartney. This pleasant-sounding, melodious and radio-friendly tune actually proved something of a minor hit, eventually peaking at #56 on the *Billboard* chart.

'Because I Love You' (Molland)
Released as a single A-side (b/w 'Too Hung Up On You'): July 1981 (US), did not chart

Molland's next writing contribution to the album offers up a wonderfully catchy pop tune reminiscent of those old 1960s female vocal groups (Joey actually likened it to The Crystals in the Cimino biography). This throwback melody, albeit filtered through Cheap Trick, was one of the numbers on the original three-track demo that got Badfinger the new record deal with Radio Records. Beautiful harmonies abound in this charming little toe-tapper, topped off by an appealing lead vocal from Joey. Disappointingly, however, as with 'I Got You', this failed to make any impression whatsoever on the singles chart.

'Rock N' Roll Contract' (Evans)
Originally written for the *Head First* album, which remained unreleased until 2000 (as detailed earlier), this remake actually ended up being the first officially released version of the song. In my opinion, this reworking actually proffers a more fully realised version than the one on *Head First* – it's faster, punchier and, ultimately, rockier than the original version. Tom's vocals still impress and the passion he exudes remains as palpable as before.

Producer Jack Richardson also found his vocal talents being called upon for this track as he was recruited to play the role of 'the manager' in the song, providing the menacing voiceover in the background. This hard-rocking number also features some blazing lead guitar solos, the first one courtesy of Joey whilst the ferocious extended solo outro is delivered by Glenn Sherba. This track was also on that original three-song demo tape sent out to the record companies in search of a new deal.

'Passin' Time' (Molland)
Exhibiting a strong Southern rock vibe, this lively, high-energy Molland-penned rocker features some sterling guitar work throughout, highlighted by a great lead solo from Glenn Sherba. Big, pounding piano chord riffs, courtesy of Tony Kaye, forcibly drive the tune along and are ably backed by Richard Bryans' solid drum beats. This great little rock song also finds Joey on fine form vocally with harmony assistance provided by Tom Evans. The bridge is rather snazzy too.

'Three Time Loser' (Molland)
Another Molland-composed number, this terrific little mid-tempo pop-rocker features a simple yet effectively catchy melody. Featuring some charming Beatles/Harrison-esque guitar throughout, this tune ably displays Joey's knack

for writing and crafting top-notch melodic pop-rock. Joey's vocals again excel and the harmonies are an utter delight too. There's also a rather appealing synthesiser solo mid-song which adds a dash of 'new wave' sound to the proceedings and enhances the overall charm of the piece. This was also the third number originally demoed and sent out to record companies in search of a new record deal.

'Too Hung Up On You' (Evans)
This Tom Evans composition is the closest thing to a traditional melancholic Badfinger ballad on the LP, but it still manages to rock out, even if it is in a more genteel fashion. Boasting an undeniably infectious refrain, this melodious retro number is both well-produced and well-sung. The musicianship is impressive throughout and the vocal harmonies remind the listener of the Badfinger of old.

'Crocadillo' (Evans, Roach)
Originally conceived as a jingle for a wine commercial in England by Tom Evans and Rod Roach, this number was transformed during the album sessions into an absolutely rollicking rocker. A nice, albeit very short, piano solo introduces the track in a rather understated fashion before the sudden sound of the full band promptly kicks in and proceeds to launch this invigoratingly energetic and compellingly catchy rock number. Electrifyingly vibrant guitar sounds propel Tom's great echoey rock vocals throughout this full-blooded piece before a sense of calm is resumed at the song's conclusion with another brief and delicate Tony Kaye piano solo.

On the original LP, this number cross-fades into the following track but on subsequent CD reissues, there is no cross-fade between the last two songs. Even stranger, the first pressing of the 2000 CD release (on Real Gone) and the 2015 Gonzo Multimedia CD reissue both reverse the playing order of the last two songs as well, with Crocadillo becoming the closing audio number (despite the printed CD tracklisting maintaining the original LP track order)!

'No More' (Molland)
The closing tinkle of piano keys from Crocadillo segues (at least on the original LP!) into the futuristic sounds of Tony Kaye's synthesiser on the record's closing track. However, before the bemused Badfinger fan can fathom out what the heck is going on, the modernistic synth bleeps give way to the reassuring sound of the full rock band. The ensuing tune is probably my overall favourite track on the album. Melding 1960s psychedelia to 'new wave' sounds, this superb Joey Molland composition features blazing guitar licks, sizzling synths and captivating vocals throughout. Joey plays the first lead guitar solo whilst Glenn Sherba delivers the absolutely blinding extended solo at the end.

Lyrically, this track finds Joey in a rather philosophical mood and he basically offers up a general commentary on the entire Badfinger story to date. His impressively moody vocal delivery is, therefore, suitably effective. In conclusion, this track essentially serves up the sonic equivalent of 'new wave' meeting The Beatles and, as such, results in a fantastic album closer!

Other Contemporary Songs
'Clouds Of Love' (Molland)
This 1980 home demo, featuring just Joey on electric guitar, closely resembles the material found on *Say No More* in that it stems from the same old-school rock 'n' roll musical template. It's a lively and catchy sounding toe-tapper and showed a lot of promise at this early demo stage. It doesn't offer anything new or improved when compared with Joey's contributions to *Say No More*, but the songwriting craft evident here is certainly equal to that which graced the released album. This demo is available on Joey's *Demo's Old and New* CD.

'When' (Molland)
Another demo stemming from 1980, this one actually finds Joey supported by a full band, including Badfinger alumnus Joe Tansin. This guitar-driven piece is yet another buoyant, catchy pop-rocker with an urgent beat. It's a great sounding song that once again showed a lot of promise and potential at this early run through stage. Again, this demo can be found on Joey's *Demo's Old and New* CD.

Epilogue

The original Radio Records contract with Badfinger had been a two-album deal, so once the *Say No More* LP's brief lifespan had run its course, the band reconvened with a view to starting work on the follow-up record. However, in a sadly predictable manner, various issues arose, which ultimately put paid to any chance of a new album being produced. It would seem that a combination of factors – including a lack of new songs/demos, an insufficient offer of advance money, etc. – all contributed to a rather acrimonious situation whereby both band and record company alike were extremely unhappy with the state of affairs.

Joey's side of the story has often been that the record company turned up and only presented the band with half of the promised advance money for the new album. He wasn't at all happy with this and subsequently withdrew from the project. However, from the record company/producer's point of view, they were incredibly unhappy with the fact that there were hardly any new songs/demos ready for a second album. Indeed, subsequent comments made by both guitarist Glenn Sherba, and keyboardist Tony Kaye, in the Dan Matovina-authored band biography would seem to bear this out. Glenn: 'When I got to rehearsals, Joey had already gone. Our producer, Jack Richardson, had come down and there weren't many songs.' Tony: 'The record company was upset. They said there better be songs before we'll let you do an album.'

Well, whatever the reasons, Joey was indeed so disgruntled with matters at the time that he refused to continue working towards a new album, duly packing up his guitar and abandoning the rehearsals entirely. According to the Michael Cimino biography, Joey thought that Tom Evans and Tony Kaye were on his side in the matter and agreed with his stance. However, he was in for a bit of a shock when Tom and Tony instead started informing everyone that Joey had actually left the band! Tom and Tony, it seemed, were intent on keeping Badfinger going without Joey, making plans to tour and still hopeful of recording a new album. Joey got wind of this and, in an effort to prevent the other two from performing as Badfinger, quickly put together his own version of the band (including former member Joe Tansin) and started touring around US clubs.

It is, therefore, not at all surprising then that, against this backdrop of turbulent turmoil, Radio Records decided not to take up the option of a second record with the band. So it was that Joey remained in the US touring with his version of Badfinger whilst Tom returned to England.

Upon his return to England, Tom initially teamed up with his old pal, Rod Roach, to work on new music, but it wasn't long before he put together another version of Badfinger. To outdo Joey, Tom managed to reunite with former Badfinger alumni Mike Gibbins and Bob Jackson, and so 1982/3 saw two competing versions of the band out on the road. In addition to all this personal and professional conflict, there were still ongoing business and financial difficulties to contend with, too, particularly the issue of frozen Apple royalties.

At one point in 1983, Tom Evans and Bob Jackson also attempted to get a new project off the ground, humorously entitled 'Goodfinger'. Some demos were done and peddled around record companies but without any success. After some further work with Rod Roach, Tom put together another version of Badfinger for an Autumn tour, this time recruiting former members Tony Kaye and Glenn Sherba to join him and Bob Jackson.

Throughout this period, Tom's problems continued to mount – financial troubles, marital problems, health issues – the drinking subsequently got heavier and the depression deepened. Tragically, as had happened earlier with Pete Ham, it all became too much for Tom to bear and on 19 November 1983, Evans hanged himself in his garden. He was just 36 years old.

Shortly after this tragedy, in early 1984, Joey Molland, Mike Gibbins and Bob Jackson toured together as Badfinger, with Joey and Mike continuing to tour together sporadically for the rest of the decade. Joey released his first solo album in 1983 and has subsequently released several other well-received solo works, the latest of which appeared in 2020. Joey also continues to tour as Joey Molland's Badfinger. Mike Gibbins released a handful of low-key solo albums during the late 1990s and early 2000s before his sad death from a brain aneurysm in 2005. In 2015, Bob Jackson formed his own touring version of Badfinger, playing the 'oldies' circuit.

Regarding the tangled web of their rather complex business and financial affairs, a legal agreement was finally reached in 1985, which saw the release and appropriate division of outstanding Apple royalty payments to Joey, Mike and the estates of Pete Ham and Tom Evans, respectively. Concerning their former business manager, Stan Polley, he was finally brought to justice in 1991 (albeit in a non-Badfinger related business matter) when he pleaded guilty to charges of misappropriating funds and money laundering. He managed to avoid a jail sentence but still ended up being put on probation for five years. Subsequently, after suffering ill health for a number of years, Polley passed away in 2009.

The 1990s saw the majority of the band's albums released on CD for the first time, many with bonus tracks (with further reissues forthcoming in the 21st Century with additional bonus tracks). 1990 also saw the release of *Day After Day – Badfinger Live*, the ten-track 'live' album sourced from the 4 March 1974 gig at the Cleveland Agora club, Ohio. As mentioned earlier, whilst oft-panned and much-maligned by fans and critics alike (due to its overuse of re-recording and overdubbing), this release from Rykodisc (co-produced by Joey Molland) is still worth seeking out due to the paucity of live Badfinger material officially available. There is still much enjoyment to be found in this release and, let's be honest, how many bands' live albums are genuinely 100% live without any sort of post-production enhancement? Not many...

However, for a more genuine live representation of the classic line-up, listeners are directed towards the 1997 Strange Fruit CD release, *BBC In Concert 1972-3*. Featuring two separate concerts recorded at the Paris Theatre,

London, these live recordings readily demonstrate how the band tended to 'rock out' a lot more in a live setting as opposed to their more polite and refined studio incarnation. In addition to the group's self-penned numbers, there are also a couple of interesting cover versions thrown in, including a couple of Dave Mason numbers (Mason had been a founding member of Traffic), namely 'Feelin' Alright' and 'Only You Know And I Know'. In 2020, there was also the semi-official/grey market Leftfield Media release of the *Kansas City 1972* CD, which allegedly presents a live FM radio broadcast of the Cowtown Ballroom gig from April 7, 1972 – to be fair, this recording is actually pretty decent sounding and offers fans another rare and valuable snapshot of the band's classic line-up in a live setting. The tracklisting also offers a handful of songs not performed on the BBC CD, including a rather fun medley of classic rock 'n' roll tunes. Late 2021 also saw the release on CD of *The Lost Broadcasts* – released on the Cantare label, this album features tracks allegedly culled from five BBC Radio One sessions and a pair of *Top of the Pops* slots. These live recordings, of varying sound quality, apparently date from 1969-70 and document the transitional period during which The Iveys morphed into Badfinger. Featuring several tracks each from both The Iveys and Badfinger, a lot of the content is made up of cover versions of songs which were probably prevalent in their live sets at the time – ranging from Soul/R&B (with covers of 'Respect', 'The Way You Do The Things You Do' and 'Just One Look') to Rock/Pop (with covers of Traffic's 'You Can All Join In', The Beatles' 'Birthday' and The Band's 'Up On Cripple Creek'). This all makes for a very interesting listen, to be sure, but it's probably one for the superfan only in all honesty (like me)!

For those who wish to investigate the live sounds of the non-classic line-ups, there have been a couple of interesting releases – 2002 saw the low-key, limited release of *DBA – BFR* (aka *Doing Business As Badfinger*) on the Exile Music label, which offers up a live concert performed in Indiana, October 1982, and features the Tom Evans/Mike Gibbins/Bob Jackson line-up. Taken from Mike Gibbins' personal collection, this gig was recorded on a consumer cassette recorder and although the sound quality isn't all that great, it still provides listeners with a rare opportunity to check out this latter-day line-up who were still evidently capable of delivering the goods in a live setting; for a taste of Joey Molland's Badfinger, there was the 2019 release (via the Gonzo Multimedia label) of *Without You*, a live recording taken from a gig in Sellersville, Philadelphia, March 2010. Perfectly listenable, this show sees Joey and assorted chums tackling a good mix of Badfinger numbers with a few of his solo tracks thrown in for good measure. Joey is in high spirits throughout and although this is hardly essential listening, it's still a fun listen.

In addition to these original album CD reissues and the sprinkling of live albums, there have also been a handful of Badfinger compilations released on CD during the 1990s and 2000s. Notable ones include *The Best Of Badfinger Volume II* (Rhino Records, 1990 – 17 tracks focussing on the Warner Brothers years with a couple of Elektra tracks thrown in for good measure), *The Best Of*

Badfinger (Apple Records, 1995 – featuring 21 tracks culled from the Apple era), *The Very Best Of Badfinger* (Apple Records, 2000 – featuring 19 tracks from both the Apple and Warner Brothers eras) and *Timeless... The Musical Legacy* (Apple Records, 2013 – a 16-track, career-spanning set which was released shortly after the warmly received use of the track 'Baby Blue' in the closing scene of the last episode of the successful US TV series *Breaking Bad*).

Two other releases bearing the Badfinger moniker (but in reality, being purely Joey Molland-led projects) are worth mentioning – released in 1995 on the Eclipse Music Group label and simply entitled *Badfinger*, this ten-track album features re-recordings performed by Joey Molland and a group of uncredited musicians. Whilst the performances are perfectly adequate, albeit perfunctory, I'm not sure what the point of this release was aside from it being a quick cash grab project for Joey; more recently, an album entitled *No Matter What – Revisiting The Hits* was released by Cleopatra Records in 2021 and features Joey Molland again re-recording ten of the band's numbers, but this time with the assistance of some high-profile musical colleagues (including, amongst others, Mark Stein, Rick Wakeman, Terry Reid, Ian Anderson, Rick Springfield, Matthew Sweet and Todd Rundgren). It certainly makes for a pleasant enough listening experience with solid performances all around, but with fairly faithful renditions that fail to outshine the original versions, one may again question the need for such a release. However, Joey should at least be applauded for his continued efforts in promoting Badfinger's musical legacy in the 21st century.

Reflecting on the band's history and legacy many years on, Joey Molland candidly expressed his feelings in an interview with *Guitar World* (October 2020):

> People say things like 'the saddest story in rock,' and I guess they always will. I can't get away from it, but I don't really dwell on it. I try to focus on the good things that we did and all the great songs we recorded. I meet people all the time who know our music. Sure, I wish things didn't turn out as they did. We had two people in the band take their own lives – that's a tragedy on a human level. Who knows what drives people to do such a thing? But I can't think about 'what might have been'. You go crazy if you live your life like that. I feel as if things could've turned out differently. If we had different management, we could have gone on. Getting involved with the crook [Stan Polley] was the worst thing we ever did. We could always write songs; we could always play. We just had bad business, and it finished us.

The Badfinger story is indeed one filled with many trials and tribulations, mishaps and misfortune, and, critically, the band are often defined as one of rock music's great tragedies. However, this should not overshadow their true legacy – the music they left behind. Although effectively cut off in their prime, Badfinger still produced a truly wonderful body of recorded work, impressively consistent in its remarkable quality.

Whilst their links (and comparisons) to The Beatles cannot be denied, this patronage proved a double-edged sword, for whilst America eagerly embraced the band in the early 1970s as successors to the throne, the British music press and public alike tended to view the band with more suspicion, generally regarding them as mere Beatles copyists. However, through their mastery of the pop idiom, Badfinger proved themselves more than simple Beatles imitators. They crafted timeless, melodic and harmonic pop-rock of the highest calibre that boasted rich, harmonious vocals, inspired arrangements and superb musicianship. Badfinger should never be forgotten and, at the very least, with the song 'Without You' having become a true classic pop standard, this alone should ensure that their musical legacy endures.

Sharing a unique, magical chemistry, the classic line-up of Pete, Tom, Joey and Mike poured their collective hearts and souls into their music and it is this honesty and passion that shines through and which has allowed their songbook to continue to resonate throughout the ensuing years. The advent of the digital age and the reissuing of their catalogue has certainly helped this cause and their music is increasingly (and rightfully) being accorded the kind of acclaim and admiration that is long overdue. It was particularly gratifying to see an example of this when the track 'Baby Blue' was used in the *Breaking Bad* TV series finale and subsequent streaming and downloading of the track went through the roof. Their music has, of course, appeared (and continues to appear) in various other high-profile TV shows and movies and their popular hits remain staples of classic rock radio.

Whilst Badfinger may have been well and truly underrated and underappreciated during their actual lifetime, it is reassuring to know that, as the years go by, their contribution to pop and rock music history is, albeit belatedly, being recognised and respected and it is immensely satisfying to know that their music continues to touch the hearts and minds of new generations of listeners.

Further Related And Recommended Albums Of Interest

Any self-respecting Badfinger fan should seek out the two Rykodisc released compilations of Pete Ham home demos – *7 Park Avenue* (1997) and *Golders Green* (1999) – within this book, I have already made reference to many of the relevant demos contained within these two releases, but there are still other musical treasures to be found on these two collections (including tracks whose date of origin couldn't be pinpointed with absolute certainty to specific album periods and other tracks which offer very brief musical snippets rather than fully-formed songs). The demos date from the late 1960s up to 1975, but it should be noted, however, that a number of the songs have been enhanced, albeit sympathetically, by new overdubs (including musical contributions from ex-Badfinger member Bob Jackson and ex-Iveys member Ron Griffiths). In 2013, there was a third release of Pete Ham home demos. Entitled *Keyhole Street: Demos 1966-67*, this was a very limited CD release (on the Without You Music label) and features two discs of interesting home demos recorded by Pete when he was just 19 and 20 years of age.

For the Tommy Evans fans out there, you should seek out the rather hard-to-find 1993 CD release (issued by Gipsy Records), *Over You (The Final Tracks)*, which features eleven unreleased demo tracks from the 1980-83 period by Tom Evans and his musical collaborator, Rod Roach. This collection provides ample evidence that Tom was still creating top-notch melodic pop songs even in the final years of his life. Also highly recommended is the 1991 *Badfinger – Apple Daze* CD released via Raven Records. This disc contains a half-hour audio interview from 1982 (between Glenn A. Baker and Tom Evans) and is subtitled *A Rare And Revealing Interview With The Late Tommy Evans Covering Badfinger, The Beatles, Apple And The Death Of The 60s*. This fantastic interview makes for an incredibly interesting and informative listen. Tom is utterly charming throughout and in noticeably good spirits, recalling the band's history with plenty of honesty, humour and pathos.

For the Joey fans out there, I would heartily recommend investigating both his solo output and the Natural Gas project. Joey, to this day, remains a torchbearer for power pop and the albums listed below reveal him to be a perennial purveyor of terrific melodic pop rock:

Joey Molland: *After The Pearl* (1983), *The Pilgrim* (1992), *Basil* (1998; reissued in 2015 with new title *Demo's Old And New*), *This Way Up* (2001), *Return To Memphis* (2013), *Be True To Yourself* (2020)

Natural Gas: *Natural Gas* (1976), *Live From The Vault (Live At Cobo Arena, Detroit, MI 1976)* (2018)

Finally, for the hardcore fans out there, there are also two limited edition CD releases available containing rare live performances of the pre-Badfinger group, The Iveys. The first of these, released in 2017, is entitled *Origins – The Iveys Anthology Vol. 1 Live At The Empire June 7, 1966 Neath, S. Wales*, whilst the second one, released in 2019, is entitled *Origins – The Iveys Anthology Vol. 2 Live At Thingamajig Club Reading U.K. Sept. 6, 1968*. Both of these rare live performances were made available by former Iveys bassist Ron Griffiths, on his RL Griffiths Presents label.

Again, for fans of The Iveys in particular, I would also recommend seeking out the following Apple-focused various artists CD compilations released in the 2000s by the RPM label: *94 Baker Street: The Pop-Psych Sounds Of The Apple Era 1967-1969* (2003), *An Apple A Day: More Pop-Psych Sounds From The Apple Era 1967-1969* (2006) and *Treacle Toffee World: Further Adventures Into The Pop-Psych Sounds From The Apple Era 1967-1969* (2008). As detailed earlier in the book, these three releases all contain a number of previously unreleased early demos by The Iveys.

Bibliography

Books

Matovina, D., *Without You: The Tragic Story of Badfinger* (Frances Glover Books, 1997; second edition 2000 – both editions came with a bonus audio CD (containing demos, interviews, etc.), although the tracklisting differed for both editions)

Cimino, M.A., *Badfinger and Beyond – The Biography of Joey Molland* (Cottage Views, 2011)

Visconti, T., *Bowie, Bolan and the Brooklyn Boy: the Autobiography* (Harper Collins Publishers, 2007)

Online Articles

Schinder, S., *Badfinger: The Triumph and Tragedy of 'The Next Beatles'* (online article, 1 October 2020, https://www.pleasekillme.com)

Heatley, M., *Badfinger: Bad Breaks, Dumb Luck and Sheer Tragedy* (online article, 24 April 2017, https://www.loudersound.com)

Badfinger (online article, https://www.thisdayinmusic.com)

Kemp, S., *The Second Beatles: The Tragic Story of Badfinger* (online article, 27 October 2021, https://faroutmagazine.co.uk)

Kopp, B., *Badfinger* (online article, 27 November 2018, https://recordcollectormag.com)

Polcaro, R., *The Tragic Story of Badfinger Deaths* (online article, 25 February 2019, http://rockandrollgarage.com)

Wood, C., *Badfinger's Last Original Member Still Playing Their Music* (online article, 30 January 2016, https://www.bbc.co.uk)

Tomlinson, G., *No Matter What / Peter Ham and Badfinger* (online article, 22 April 2014, https://www.walesartsreview.org)

Owens, D., *Badfinger Musician is Hoping to Reclaim the Welsh Group's Songs from Their Tragic Past* (online article, 12 December 2016, https://www.walesonline.co.uk)

Badfinger 1970 Albums (online article, 25 May 2015, https://www.classicrockreview.com)

Badfinger (online article, https://nostalgiacentral.com)

Brandon, G., *The Dramatic Conclusion of Badfinger... And the Lost Album You've Never Heard of* (online article, http://www.rebeatmag.com)

Barnard, J., *Bob Jackson – Badfinger* (online article, 2016, https://thestrangebrew.co.uk)

Fiedler, J., *Discog Fever – Rating and Reviewing Every Badfinger Album* (online article, 19 October 2016, http://www.thegreatalbums.com)

Bosso, J., *Badfinger's Joey Molland on The Beatles, Apple Records Reissues and Tragedy* (online article, 21 November 2010, https://www.musicradar.com)

The Story of Badfinger and Their Supposed to be Success (online article, https://societyofrock.com)

Rock N Roll Suicide: Pete Ham & Tom Evans of Badfinger Can't Take It Anymore (online article, 5 March 2012, https://lonesomebeehive.com)

DeRiso, N., *Why Badfinger Fell Apart with the Failure of 'Wish You Were Here'* (online article, 28 November 2014, https://ultimateclassicrock.com)

Rock Band Tragedy: A 'Soulless Bastard' Manager Caused Two Suicides (online article, https://billmichelmore.com)

Deb, A., *Badfinger – A Rock and Roll Tragedy* (online article, 28 August 2020, https://thatguyavik.medium.com)

Bosso, J., *Joey Molland Looks Back on Badfinger's Tumultuous, Remarkable Career – 50 Years On* (online article, 21 October 2020, https://www.guitarworld.com)

Badfinger (online article, https://thevogue.com)

Elijah, D., *Badfinger's Career was Plagued by Death, Robbery, and Turmoil* (online article, 2019, https://rockmusicrevival.com)

Elbel, J., *Badfinger – Self-titled, Wish You Were Here (Real Gone)* (online article, 18 January 2019, https://bigtakeover.com)

Marchese, J., *Review: The Apple Records Remasters, Part 1 – A Quartet by Badfinger* (online article, 15 November 2010, https://theseconddisc.com)

Sawdey, E., *Badfinger – Wish You Were Here* (online article, 24 October 2007, https://www.popmatters.com)

Greenblatt, M., *Whether it was Bad Luck, Bad Karma or Bad Timing, Badfinger Met a Bad End* (online article, 6 August 2014, https://www.goldminemag.com)

Fortes, M., *The Popdose Guide to Badfinger* (online article, 15 April 2008, https://popdose.com)

Janowsky, S., *The Life and Death of 'Badfinger'* (online article, 3 August 2009, https://reviewfix.com)

Hall, R., *Badfinger 'Straight Up': A Power Pop Masterpiece* (online article, https://bestclassicbands.com)

Toth, E., *Joey Molland, The TVD Interview* (online article, 16 October 2020, https://www.thevinyldistrict.com)

Perry, S., *The Joey Molland Interview* (online article, https://vintagerock.com)

Mastropolo, F., *I'm Still Standing: Joey Molland Transcends Badfinger's Tragic Past with Latest Album, 'Be True To Yourself'* (online article, 12 October 2020, https://www.rockcellarmagazine.com)

Rowland, H., *A Conversation with Joey Molland (Badfinger)* (online article, 21 October 2020, https://magnetmagazine.com)

Joey Molland of Badfinger (online article, 5 April 2018, https://crypticrock.com)

Barnard, J., *Joey Molland – From Liverpool to Memphis* (online article, 2014, https://thestrangebrew.co.uk)

Zabielski, D., *Finding the Good in Badfinger's History: A Conversation with Joey Molland* (online article, 3 March 2017, http://www.rebeatmag.com)

Lyng, E., *Badfinger: A Conversation with Chris Thomas* (online article, 28 April 2019, www.culturesonar.com)
Truslow, N., *Management, Music, and Misery: Badfinger Signs Their Life Away* (online article, 2 January 2015, www.nedrock.org)
Interview with...Joe Tansin (online article, 20 August 2013, www.interviewswithrawkinrik.wordpress.com)
An Interview with Bob Jackson of Badfinger (online article, 2016, www.bandonthewall.org)

Websites
www.badfingerlibrary.com (online resource – highly recommended)
https://www.facebook.com/groups/2211874004/ (Badfinger Facebook group)
http://badfinger.publog.jp/ (online resource)
https://www.rocksbackpages.com (online archive of music journalism)
https://justbackdated.blogspot.com/ (a blog by music journalist Chris Charlesworth)
www.superseventies.com (online resource which includes archival album reviews)
https://www.allmusic.com (online music resource)
https://www.angelfire.com/nv/Badfinger (online resource)
https://forums.stevehoffman.tv (this online music forum contains many, many Badfinger discussion threads covering various topics!)

TV/DVD Documentaries
Badfinger documentary, *Week In, Week Out*, BBC Wales, 1987 (available on YouTube)
Badfinger – A Riveting and Emotionally Gripping Saga DVD, 1997
Badfinger special, *Behind the Music*, VH1, 2000 (available on YouTube)
Badfinger, *Jukebox Heroes*, BBC, 2002 (available on YouTube)
Badfinger special, *They Sold a Million*, BBC Wales, 2014 (available on YouTube)

CD Liner Notes
CD liner notes from all the various Badfinger (and related) CD album reissues/compilations that have been released.

Also available from Sonicbond

On Track series

Alan Parsons Project – Steve Swift 978-1-78952-154-2

Tori Amos – Lisa Torem 978-1-78952-142-9

Asia – Peter Braidis 978-1-78952-099-6

Badfinger – Robert Day-Webb 978-1-878952-176-4

Barclay James Harvest – Keith and Monica Domone 978-1-78952-067-5

The Beatles – Andrew Wild 978-1-78952-009-5

The Beatles Solo 1969-1980 – Andrew Wild 978-1-78952-030-9

Blue Oyster Cult – Jacob Holm-Lupo 978-1-78952-007-1

Blur – Matt Bishop 978-178952-164-1

Marc Bolan and T.Rex – Peter Gallagher 978-1-78952-124-5

Kate Bush – Bill Thomas 978-1-78952-097-2

Camel – Hamish Kuzminski 978-1-78952-040-8

Caravan – Andy Boot 978-1-78952-127-6

Cardiacs – Eric Benac 978-1-78952-131-3

Eric Clapton Solo – Andrew Wild 978-1-78952-141-2

The Clash – Nick Assirati 978-1-78952-077-4

Crosby, Stills and Nash – Andrew Wild 978-1-78952-039-2

The Damned – Morgan Brown 978-1-78952-136-8

Deep Purple and Rainbow 1968-79 – Steve Pilkington 978-1-78952-002-6

Dire Straits – Andrew Wild 978-1-78952-044-6

The Doors – Tony Thompson 978-1-78952-137-5

Dream Theater – Jordan Blum 978-1-78952-050-7

Electric Light Orchestra – Barry Delve 978-1-78952-152-8

Elvis Costello and The Attractions – Georg Purvis 978-1-78952-129-0

Emerson Lake and Palmer – Mike Goode 978-1-78952-000-2

Fairport Convention – Kevan Furbank 978-1-78952-051-4

Peter Gabriel – Graeme Scarfe 978-1-78952-138-2

Genesis – Stuart MacFarlane 978-1-78952-005-7

Gentle Giant – Gary Steel 978-1-78952-058-3

Gong – Kevan Furbank 978-1-78952-082-8

Hall and Oates – Ian Abrahams 978-1-78952-167-2

Hawkwind – Duncan Harris 978-1-78952-052-1

Peter Hammill – Richard Rees Jones 978-1-78952-163-4

Roy Harper – Opher Goodwin 978-1-78952-130-6

Jimi Hendrix – Emma Stott 978-1-78952-175-7

The Hollies – Andrew Darlington 978-1-78952-159-7

Iron Maiden – Steve Pilkington 978-1-78952-061-3

Jefferson Airplane – Richard Butterworth 978-1-78952-143-6

Jethro Tull – Jordan Blum 978-1-78952-016-3

Elton John in the 1970s – Peter Kearns 978-1-78952-034-7

The Incredible String Band – Tim Moon 978-1-78952-107-8

Iron Maiden – Steve Pilkington 978-1-78952-061-3

Judas Priest – John Tucker 978-1-78952-018-7

Kansas – Kevin Cummings 978-1-78952-057-6

The Kinks – Martin Hutchinson 978-1-78952-172-6

Korn – Matt Karpe 978-1-78952-153-5

Led Zeppelin – Steve Pilkington 978-1-78952-151-1

Level 42 – Matt Philips 978-1-78952-102-3

Little Feat – 978-1-78952-168-9

Aimee Mann – Jez Rowden 978-1-78952-036-1

Joni Mitchell – Peter Kearns 978-1-78952-081-1

The Moody Blues – Geoffrey Feakes 978-1-78952-042-2

Motorhead – Duncan Harris 978-1-78952-173-3

Mike Oldfield – Ryan Yard 978-1-78952-060-6

Opeth – Jordan Blum 978-1-78-952-166-5

Tom Petty – Richard James 978-1-78952-128-3

Porcupine Tree – Nick Holmes 978-1-78952-144-3

Queen – Andrew Wild 978-1-78952-003-3

Radiohead – William Allen 978-1-78952-149-8

Renaissance – David Detmer 978-1-78952-062-0

The Rolling Stones 1963-80 – Steve Pilkington 978-1-78952-017-0

The Smiths and Morrissey – Tommy Gunnarsson 978-1-78952-140-5

Status Quo the Frantic Four Years – Richard James 978-1-78952-160-3

Steely Dan – Jez Rowden 978-1-78952-043-9

Steve Hackett – Geoffrey Feakes 978-1-78952-098-9

Thin Lizzy – Graeme Stroud 978-1-78952-064-4

Toto – Jacob Holm-Lupo 978-1-78952-019-4

U2 – Eoghan Lyng 978-1-78952-078-1

UFO – Richard James 978-1-78952-073-6

The Who – Geoffrey Feakes 978-1-78952-076-7

Roy Wood and the Move – James R Turner 978-1-78952-008-8

Van Der Graaf Generator – Dan Coffey 978-1-78952-031-6

Yes – Stephen Lambe 978-1-78952-001-9

Frank Zappa 1966 to 1979 – Eric Benac 978-1-78952-033-0

Warren Zevon – Peter Gallagher 978-1-78952-170-2

10CC – Peter Kearns 978-1-78952-054-5